BookBub Ads Expert

A Marketing Guide to Author Discovery

David Gaughran lives in Dublin, where rain comes up from the ground and everyone has pints for hands. He writes historical fiction (and science fiction under another name), and has helped thousands of authors publish their work through his workshops, blog, and writers' books: *Let's Get Digital*, *Strangers to Superfans*, and *Amazon Decoded*. He has also created giant marketing campaigns for some of the biggest indies on the planet, and has been featured in the *Telegraph*, the *Irish Times*, the *Guardian*, the *Irish Examiner*, the *Sunday Times*, *Huffington Post*, *Techdirt*, *Business Insider*, *Forbes*, *The Verge*, *Re/Code*, *Bustle*, *Inc*, *Mashable*, *Pajiba*, several Wanted posters in the Tri-State area, *TechCrunch*, *Newsweek Polska*, *il Giornale*, *The Star Malaysia*, and—most pleasingly—the *Journal for Maritime Research*.

Praise for *A Storm Hits Valparaiso*

"An ambitious story of love and betrayal, victory and defeat. In characters drawn from real historical figures, the author delves into the politics of war and how battles turn on the smallest of details or the whims of a single man."
—JW Manus, author of *The Devil His Due*.

"A work of sweeping historical fiction that captivates and entertains … engaging and richly textured."
—John D. Glass, author of *Legend of Zodiac*

Praise for *Mercenary*

"Highly recommended to readers of adventure fiction and history, as well as anyone interested in American adventurism and meddling in Latin America."
—*Wall Street Journal* and *USA Today* bestselling author Michael Wallace

"Lee Christmas led a roaring life on and off the battlefield. Gaughran's great, fast-paced read keeps you right alongside all his exploits."
—Richard Sutton, author of *The Red Gate*

Praise for *Liberty Boy:*

"Liberty Boy is a riveting tale of an overlooked rebellion, told from the perspective of the streets, with gifted dialogue that is more heard than read and unexpected twists that leave you breathless from first page to last."
—Cindy Vallar, *Historical Novels Review*

ISBN: 978-91-87109-27-0

Editor: Tammi Labrecque
Cover: Alexios Saskalidis, 187Designz
Formatting: Paul Salvette, BB eBooks

Published February 2019

DavidGaughran.com

A MARKETING GUIDE
TO AUTHOR DISCOVERY

BOOKBUB
ADS EXPERT

DAVID GAUGHRAN

CONTENTS

Introduction

BookBub launched in 2012 and quickly set about transforming the book discovery landscape. Multiple options already existed for authors and publishers to promote discounts, but BookBub took things to the next level in terms of presentation, execution, and—most importantly—results; soon the power of one BookBub Featured Deals promotion exceeded all other such discount sites. Combined.

It's easy to see why BookBub exploded in popularity. Several years ago, I signed up to BookBub's daily Featured Deals email, the first I'd seen where you could indicate specific genre preferences—and in quite a granular sense too. Prefer Dark Romance over something lighter or sweeter? Want Advice/How To books but have little interest in Business or Cooking? BookBub allowed readers that granularity of choice. It also helped that the offers themselves were genuinely noteworthy—a nice mix of generous discounts from familiar names and price drops encouraging you to try undiscovered gems, in each of the genres you chose, at free or 99¢. (Although the prices of these discounted books have been creeping up recently: in many genres, $1.99 is more common now than 99¢ or free, and even $2.99 is making an appearance for the biggest titles from large publishers.)

Getting a BookBub Featured Deal used to involve simply applying for one; with professional presentation and some nice reviews, your chances of acceptance were pretty good, and then you could look forward to hundreds of sales on the day of your promotion. It's now *significantly* harder to get a Featured Deal. While subscriber numbers have grown spectacularly, there is still only one Featured Deals email a day, meaning that demand now far outstrips supply. But the flipside is this: if you're selected, that incredible audience growth means you can sell *thousands* of books on promo day, enjoy increased sales and visibility for a sustained period afterwards, and experience ancillary benefits too—like more robust sell-through and mailing list sign-ups.

BookBub has millions of readers on its various genre-specific mailing lists now, a passionate and diverse community of book buyers—and that last word, *buyers*, is crucial. Goodreads, for example, has an even bigger community of book *lovers* but has singularly failed to build a way for advertisers (i.e.

gatecrashers like you and me) to monetize that passion effectively.

I suppose the second-to-last word back there—*book*—is pretty crucial too. Facebook is a massive advertising platform that's incredibly effective at reaching people; it feels like half the world is a regular Facebook user... because they are. But it's a generalized audience and we must pan for readers in that fast-flowing stream. Same goes for Google Ads—except there is no reader-gold!

With the benefit of hindsight, I guess it was inevitable that BookBub would set up an ad platform. BookBub invested more aggressively than anyone else in that space, allowing it to execute its offer in a much slicker way. Social media, graphic design, branding, content marketing—that investment gave it a real edge, but also created a very valuable audience that could be served (and monetized) in other ways. The exponential growth in its audience was matched by demand from authors and publishers to reach those readers, and BookBub met that demand by expanding its services.

Featured Deals are still remarkably effective, and remain extremely popular with readers, but they have now been augmented by several other products. Some are free—like New Release Alerts, which are very effective and don't cost a penny. Others are paid services, like Pre-Order Alerts and the focus of this book: BookBub Ads.

In addition, BookBub has been gradually pivoting for some time now from being an email-focused company to also having a strong emphasis on its website, building an online destination for readers with social aspects, kind of like a more modern, retailer-agnostic version of Goodreads. BookBub is encouraging users to leave reviews on its site and follow their favorite authors, who are encouraged in turn to recommend books to their reader-followers.

BookBub wants its site to be a place where readers hang out. Where this becomes particularly relevant is that all this site-based activity—and the email alerts it generates—greatly increase the potential exposure of BookBub Ads. Remember, these aren't just delivered underneath Featured Deal emails, but also in emails like New Release Alerts and recommendations from authors you follow. The number of notifications being sent out every day has risen dramatically over the last year, which in turn has greatly expanded the reach of the ad platform, seemingly without any drag on performance either. And that's before we get into the new placement of BookBub Ads on the site itself.

What all this means is that BookBub Ads is about to *explode*.

In one sense, it's such a simple system. However, embracing the quirks of the platform will lead you to truly master it. That dimension is crucial because BookBub can be one of the most unforgiving environments around for novices. The ad interface is considerably less intimidating than Facebook or Amazon, but this leads many to underestimate the level of complexity under the hood and make critical mis-steps. The margins between success and failure are wafer-thin, leading many to walk away very frustrated indeed.

But they are quitting too soon. Because if you take the time to perfect your images and targeting, you will nail down the quickest and most effective way to reach millions of passionate readers that has ever existed. And the time to become a *BookBub Ads Expert* is now.

I've managed major BookBub Ads campaigns across a number of genres. Aside from my own books, I've run ads for a string of *New York Times* and *USA Today* bestselling authors and have watched the platform explode, over the last twelve months in particular. BookBub Ads used to be a nice bolt-on to any launch or promotion, but they have now become one of the main drivers. To my amazement, BookBub Ads can be just as effective at reaching readers at scale as Facebook Ads, beats the pants off Amazon Ads in every metric, and convert far better than either of them.

Many authors try the platform half-heartedly, and invariably fail—so if *you* take the time to master it, you'll have a serious competitive advantage. We'll cover everything you need to know in this one book. I'm not trying to sell you a course or a webinar where all the *real* info exits. All my secrets are here.

Well, except for that one time I experimented in college…

Dublin, February 2019

PART I

BOOKBUB BASICS

This section will walk you through the basics of BookBub Ads. Find out how the platform works, the process through which ads are served, what makes BookBub Ads very different indeed, and all the ways you can exploit those differences to get better results. But that sounds boring, so let's sex it up a bit: this part will make you RICH! Okay, overshot the runway a little there; let me rein it in a touch: this section will make you smarter about how the system works. Then we'll build on that knowledge to make you... oh, you'll see. (Spoiler: it involves money raining on your face.)

1: How BookBub Ads Work

To be successful with BookBub Ads, you must first understand how they are served to readers, because the system operates very differently than Facebook or Amazon Ads—or indeed any other platform out there you might be familiar with. For starters, BookBub Ads are almost exclusively served to readers via email, rather than on a website or social network. While BookBub has begun serving *some* ads on their website also, this won't change the predominant action happening via emails to readers. This isn't just an academic point; how the ads are delivered influences when the ads get served to readers (mostly right after the daily email is sent) as well as how they perform (success usually involves offering a discount of some description).

Ads in emails will be the driving force of any campaign, and considerably more effective than the alternative; I don't expect this situation to change. Aside from the fact that they go out to millions and millions of power readers every day—and will thus be seen by many times more readers than are browsing a particular page on the BookBub site—email ads are generally much more effective than display ads. Knowing a little about these emails, thinking about how these ads are served, and optimizing your approach accordingly will pay giant dividends to anyone using BookBub Ads.

Which means you must understand a little about how Featured Deals work, because that's generally where your ads will be served—at the bottom of Featured Deals emails. And that has one immediately obvious side-effect: unless you are also offering some sort of attractive discount, you're going to struggle.

What Are Featured Deals?

Featured Deals—a selection of carefully curated books that are either free or heavily discounted, emailed to millions of readers every day in their chosen genres— are the primary service offered to BookBub readers, and the main product offered to BookBub advertisers. And they are amazing, for both readers and authors. The power of a Featured Deal isn't just unmatched elsewhere, it's probably more than four times as powerful as the *combined* competition.

That said, they do have a few disadvantages, of sorts.

First, their unique power—while most welcome— is not exactly a boon to careful planners. If you have read *Amazon Decoded*, you'll already know that four or five days of consistent sales is what gets Amazon selling a book for you. (And if you haven't read *Amazon Decoded*, it's a free download from my website, *DavidGaughran.com*. I strongly recommend you do that before spending any real money trying to get Amazon sales going. I will probably mention this again, as it's so important. You have been warned!)

A Featured Deal delivers a huge spike in sales, but it's one that can't be matched elsewhere, meaning your book can fall as quickly as it rose, because you will struggle to keep up anything like that level of sales over several days. That's not to say it's a *bad* thing. Having to deal with an outsized sales spike is definitely a top-quality problem! But it's something that must be navigated nonetheless.

Second, quite obviously, getting a Featured Deal is outside of your control. Featured Deals are heavily curated and, according to BookBub, fewer than 20% of applicants are accepted (a lot fewer, if you ask me—particularly for paid deals on the bigger lists). Million-selling authors are rejected all the time. *New York Times* bestsellers, genuine "name" authors… it's tough to get picked (but not impossible, even for newbies). Which means you can't legitimately make it part of your planning. Suzanne Collins and Gillian Flynn probably have a *slightly* better than 20% chance of getting accepted, meaning you and I likely face longer odds. And that's before you consider books that are exclusive to Amazon, which BookBub rarely selects. Considering all that together, the challenge starts to crystallize.

Featured Deals are spectacular; that's not in question. But being selected isn't something you can rely upon—which is anathema to planning. And there are restrictions on how often you can be selected even if you are lucky enough to be picked. BookBub Ads, on the other hand, are an open platform you can use any time you like. Once you have optimized ads, it's a very reliable one too.

Where BookBub Ads Are Served

All this is particularly relevant here because that Featured Deals email is the primary place where BookBub Ads get served, and this affects everything. If you advertise on Amazon, the number of impressions your ad receives will largely depend on how many people are searching for the keywords you have chosen, or how many people are visiting the associated product pages related to those keywords. Facebook is similar in that the amount of exposure your ad will get is dependent on how many users have the interest you are targeting, or the demographic features you have selected (as well as how many are online… and how many of those you can afford to reach).

I'm in danger of hiring Muddy Waters to ghost-write this book, so I'd better crack on and tell you what's weird about BookBub Ads in particular: they primarily get served when someone opens an email from BookBub. I think we know this subconsciously but don't consider all the implications. For example, one knock-on effect is that peak serving of ads happens right when Featured Deals emails are sent, and then falls dramatically hour by hour from that point.

The other huge effect of being served in this manner is that your ad usually appears at the end of a list of top-quality books, some from huge names, in all conceivable genres, for prices as low as *free*. In other words, you're facing some stiff competition for reader attention, which results in an uphill battle if you aren't also featuring a steep discount. File that nugget away for later.

How BookBub Ads Are Served

You know *where* ads are served but how does the system decide which ad to show readers? Well, it depends on a few variables. "Hold on!" I hear you cry, from all the way over here. "I don't want all this wiffle-piffle. I just need a simple breakdown of what ads work. Stop wasting my damn—"

Well, hello Donna.

I could give you a simple template. In fact, here's one from my website: *bit.ly/BookBub1*. (Note: there will be some online tools and resources mentioned in this book. Where the real link is unmanageable, I'll use a customized *bit.ly* link so you have something easy to work with. Just remember these links are case-sensitive.) If that's what you're after, then click that link and ditch this book and slavishly copy that formula, and you might do okay... for a bit. At best. If you have a little more patience, you'll get a deep understanding of the whole system, so you'll have several such tactics at your fingertips *and* know when to cycle through them depending on your strategic needs. This patient approach is worth it. Pinky swear!

Now that Donna has been sedated, with reassur-ances, let me continue by stressing a huge advantage of how BookBub ads are served: this clumping of impressions makes it the most responsive ad platform out there. And it's not even close.

If you want to show your book to 20,000 bona fide Romantic Suspense fans, exclusively, over the space of a single morning, BookBub is pretty much the only platform that can generate such an immediate response. This key feature—responsiveness—is what really sets it apart from Facebook and Amazon Ads, its two primary competitors for author dollars.

However, this extreme responsiveness (and immediate scalability) also creates dangers. Those of you who created your first campaigns before reading this book will, no doubt, nod sagely here; money can disappear very quickly on BookBub if you are not careful. The platform will spend whatever amount you allot it, and can do so in the blink of an eye if you have your ad running when those daily emails go out. Those more used to the initial sluggishness of Facebook or the tardy reporting of Amazon Ads will get a shock when first dealing with BookBub.

And it won't be a pleasant experience for many, I suspect, as it takes quite a bit of iteration to get an effective ad on BookBub. It's totally worth the effort, though, because when you finally nail it down, it's like a cash-spewing fire hydrant. I don't know why money always gushes in all directions in these metaphors of mine, rather than arriving calmly at my door like a box of clouds being delivered by a snail, but there you go.

The BookBub Auction

That's the how and the why, but what about the which? Two things determine this: bids and targeting. We'll talk bids later; the only thing I'll quickly note right now is that there is just one ad slot in each email. It often pays to be aggressive with bids—for limited-time promos, at least. Those always-on, drip-style campaigns can ease off the throttle a little and find pockets of better value when everyone else is a busted flush. And if none of that makes sense, don't worry, it will all be explained.

For the moment, let's assume that bid of yours is aggressive and you have bullied everyone else out of the auction. (I'll also go through this in detail later.) The remaining variable is your targeting—and you have two key options: author and genre.

I'll give you lots of ways to determine and test your ideal author targets in subsequent chapters. What I want to outline at this preliminary stage is how the system functions. BookBub encourages readers to "follow" any author of their choosing—remember how I said they were building a destination for readers? If you are an author of Fantasy and choose Neil Gaiman as an author target because you aim for similar readers, your ad will be shown to all 268,533 of his followers, presuming you have the (considerable) budget needed for such coverage—and assuming Neil Gaiman's followers open their emails on the day you are advertising, because that's how most ads are delivered, lest you forget *on pain of death*.

But you can also target by genre. For example, there are 1.87m people on the Fantasy list, but that's an incredibly broad audience and it would be prohibitively expensive to reach all those people, with terrible results too, indubitably.

A more useful way to employ genre targeting is in combination with author targeting, in a kind of filtering capacity. This can be great for handling multi-genre authors like Stephen Donaldson, who writes both Epic Fantasy and Space Opera, and allows you to target the subset of his readers who will best respond to your work.

This kind of filtering is also useful for winnowing down the audience of huge trad authors. Returning to our example of Neil Gaiman—who resolutely refuses to stay in his lane, turning out Fantasy, YA, Poetry, graphic novels, Children's books, and non-fiction about Duran Duran—using genre filtering kills two birds with one stone: it drills down to that subset of readers we really need to target *and* brings the audience down to a more manageable size.

So that's the basics on how the system works—quirks, pitfalls, and opportunities. Next, we are going to talk about how BookBub Ads fit into your overall strategic plan, before explaining the key elements of a great ad.

2: General Strategy

I know you're dying to jump in, but that Future Money isn't going anywhere, so sit tight. We're going to talk strategy before getting into the ad-making nitty gritty. For those tempted to skip ahead, a warning: I'm less avant-garde than my luxurious mustache might suggest; the information is in this order for a reason. If you're one of those cats who rejects the orthodoxy of chapters, I dig your literary anarchy. But take a vacation from yourself! Wish I could, but I have this book to—ahem.

Strategy. Let's do this.

BookBub Ads can be a little weird at times, but I really like them. I use them to strategically boost launches and promote backlist, and I've also run huge BookBub campaigns for some bestselling authors. There are all sorts of ways to use the platform but the ways you can screw it up are equally numerous. A strategic approach is strongly recommended here, and the first step is knowing what you want to achieve.

Top Uses for BookBub Ads

While getting your hands dirty can be the best way to learn anything—with the possible exception of laser eye surgery—I should talk a little about how I use BookBub Ads before walking you through the process of making killer ads. The suggestions I make will be much more understandable if you know what the goal is.

There are many possible ways to use BookBub Ads; the platform is far more flexible than the simple interface might suggest:

1. **Supporting Launches.** The most obvious way to help a new release is to throw some advertising at it. While BookBub readers strongly prefer steep discounts, there are ways to push a higher priced book to this audience. And, of course, your own followers will be far less price-sensitive than a new-to-you reader. That said, authors may get more mileage from using BookBub Ads to promote backlist instead and generate spillover to the book they are launching—discounting an earlier book in the same series being a classic example.

2. **Backlist Price Promotions.** Running a discount or making a book free for a few days is still one of the most effective ways of boosting sales—both on the discounted book and subsequent books in the series—but these days a price promotion really needs ad support if it is to make any impact. However, clever use of ads can lead to really stunning results with this simple strategy.

3. **Creating an International Audience.** BookBub Ads is the easiest and cheapest way to reach readers outside of America at any kind of scale. While it is possible, of course, to use Facebook to reach international readers, it can be very difficult to get ads to serve in smaller international markets while also paired with author/genre targeting, particularly outside the most popular niches. BookBub Ads makes this very simple, allowing you to run ads to Canada, Australia, India, and the United Kingdom as well as the USA, targeting any of the authors in its extensive database. Which allows you to aggressively build up your readership in international markets which are less price-sensitive, more deal-starved, and often considerably cheaper to reach, in case that cake needs any more cherries.

4. **Going Wide.** Each market is pretty much distinct—and that goes for retailers as well as territories. If you have decided to leave Kindle Unlimited and go "wide" with your books, you need some kind of plan to reach readers at all these stores, as your book won't get magically discovered there either. In fact, discoverability is often more challenging outside of Amazon, meaning you have to be yet more proactive. Luckily, BookBub Ads is a pretty handy way of reaching readers at Apple, Barnes & Noble, Kobo, and Google, as well as all the respective international markets they operate in. If you only want to run a campaign targeting Kobo owners in Australia or Apple users in the UK, for example, BookBub Ads allows you that kind of granularity in your targeting.

5. **Pushing a Permafree.** It's not all challenges for "wide" authors, there are plenty of opportunities too. One tactic they lean heavily on is making the first book in a series permanently cheap or free (the latter being something you can't do if you are exclusive to Amazon with that book). There are a variety of tools you can use to push a permafree, and BookBub Ads is particularly effective for

running ads constantly in the background to feed new readers into your series around the world, at multiple retailers.

6. **Opting For Exclusivity.** Alternatively, enrolling in Kindle Unlimited means you have access to a bunch of new toys, such as Kindle Countdown Deals. The 70% royalty you get during such promotions is such a game-changer when it comes to advertising. For best results, take an approach similar to authors going wide and treat this as a launch, of sorts. While you can't target Kindle Unlimited subscribers directly—that goes for any platform—the best way of reaching them is focusing on achieving visibility on Amazon. Ad-backed Countdown Deals and free days are a very effective way of boosting your visibility—and not just temporarily.

7. **Solidifying Also Boughts.** We are becoming increasingly aware of how influential algorithms have become. On Amazon—the most algorithmically-driven retailer by far—nailing down appropriate Also Boughts for your book is hugely important, especially for a new release—a way of "training" Amazon's algorithms and

ensuring its system has an accurate idea of what kind of book this is, and which readers should enjoy it. Running BookBub Ads to carefully selected target authors is one of the most effective tools for solidifying your Also Boughts in this manner.

You will learn about all the above in much more detail, of course. I just wanted to show you a few basic uses for BookBub Ads, as many of these will require using the platform slightly differently to get best results. And you will also hear about much more sophisticated uses too, like boosting sell-through, turbocharging series sales, and leapfrogging TBR piles.

Before that, let's look at what makes a successful ad.

3: Two (Or Three) Ingredients For Success

We've gone through the very basics of how BookBub Ads work and highlighted some quirks of the platform—which can give you a competitive advantage if you understand and embrace them—and some *initial* strategy considerations, all to give necessary context for what's to come. BookBub Ads are simple on the surface, but mastering the platform requires knowing what's going on behind the wizard's curtain.

The basic formula for success is straightforward. It's about two things primarily: image and targeting. Well, three things—bidding is important too. But if you listen to me and focus almost exclusively on CPM Bidding, it doesn't matter so much what crazy-ass bids you put in because the image and targeting will be so good the ad will work anyway. And by "work" I mean "deliver cheap enough clicks of actual buyers from your target audience to enable you to scale up the campaign considerably and make a real impact on your promotion." Which is why I used that one-word substitute. Who has the time?

OK, so we'll go through the two—I mean three—ingredients to BookBub success very superficially first, and then really dive into each element. Let's start with images, as that's where most people veer into the ditch.

Well, it's in the top three anyway…

Image Basics

A major quirk of the BookBub Ads platform is that it's image-only. There's no ad text accompanying the visual, like with Facebook or Amazon Ads. The image—which you supply unless you foolishly use the in-built image generator—will be all the reader sees, unless they click on it, of course.

What makes them do that?

Good question, aggregated reader-person! While the image is doing all the work here in enticing readers, there are no text restrictions like on Facebook. This means you have total freedom to talk about your offer in the image itself—which you should do. Every good ad needs an offer of some kind to the eyeballs looking at it, whether represented textually or visually. Most authors understand that part, but they can also lose the run of themselves and go crazy with the text, leading to a visual muddle with no clear overarching message, especially for the fast-scrolling reader. This is often compounded by sub-par design.

That's a diplomatic way of saying your ads suck.

And they need to be *great*. Margins are tight here. When you get to the testing phase, you will see for yourself how one little graphical tweak or a slight adjustment in targeting can generate a radical improvement in performance, turning a money-torching ad into a cash-hoovering winner.

We'll dig more specifically into the elements that make a great ad image in a bit, but I want to give you the broad strokes first. You need:

- an offer—this is a deal-hungry crowd;
- pro design—this is an unforgiving environment; and,
- to kill your design darlings—we'll return to that grisly theme momentarily.

Targeting Basics

The targeting system might seem crude at first glance—to Facebook veterans in particular—but it still needs a little finessing to get good results. You really have two basic options: targeting by author or targeting by genre. The most elementary mistake here is to think this is a binary choice. Use both.

You should always target by genre. Many authors, such as myself, write in more than one. If that doesn't describe you personally, then the phenomenon might be more widespread than you realize. Filtering by genre ensures that you only show your book to the right segment of any target author's audience. But it's not only useful when targeting more omnivorous authors. Including genre targeting, even when targeting authors who write exclusively in one category, can keep your ad focused on the core fans—especially important when targeting traditionally published authors with huge followings.

For example, millions of people have read Harry Potter, without it leading to a full-on Fantasy craze. Untold numbers of readers have paged through one of John Grisham's legal thrillers without developing a wider taste for the niche. Moviegoers may have been curious about the source material behind Jurassic Park, Blade Runner, or the Da Vinci Code, and could conceivably become genuine fans of Michael Crichton, Philip K. Dick, and Dan Brown respectively, without being converted into proper fans of the wider genres. And there are more than enough true fans out there to focus your ad dollars exclusively on them.

In short, big authors can have a lot of casual fans who may not be the most profitable targets, and this is a good way of weeding them out.

Just make sure to also target by author. This isn't the place to get into a digression on the basic principles of digital marketing, but I suggest you read this article about the importance of granular targeting—*bit.ly/BookBub2*—if you need further convincing. Or if you prefer, you can just take my word that drilling down, versus targeting broadly, almost always gets you better results with online advertising.

BookBub allows you to target by author, using an exhaustive database. You still have a fair bit of legwork ahead of you to identify suitable author targets, though; BookBub doesn't currently do a great job of presenting this data in the ad interface. However, it does have more usable information on the reader side of the BookBub website—*bit.ly/BookBub3*.

Two quick things to note though. First, you will only be able to access this information if you have a *reader* account with BookBub, so if that's not the case, remedy that right away. And sign up for the Featured Deals newsletter too, so you can see how ads are delivered. Second, not everyone internationally will see the most up to date iteration of the BookBub website (at the time of writing, I believe those in Canada and the UK are still getting the older version, for example). If some of the features I describe below aren't available to you right now, don't worry; they're coming.

The reader side of BookBub may be unfamiliar to you, so take some time to look around. I'll point out some things you should pay attention to. The search bar in the top-right of the screen is a very useful little research tool. You can slot in the name of any author you like and, even before you complete your search, a handy little preview will pop up telling you how many BookBub followers they have. You can also actually complete the search and get taken to a page showing all their books and so on; this is just a little quicker if you are working through a list of potential author targets (which you will be, if I have any say in the matter!).

For example, if I input the name of Louis de Bernières—a favorite of mine and a giant in my genre—the preview tells me right away that he has just 315 followers. How can this be? He's a *bona fide* international bestseller, a deserved winner of multiple, prestigious awards and even had one of his books made into a highly publicized Hollywood movie starring Nicholas Cage and Penelope Cruz. Even though Louis de Bernières has probably sold a hundred times as many books as me, and even though he is most certainly a far superior novelist, I have significantly more followers. This apparent disparity is explained by how those followers are generated—largely a function of how many Featured Deals or BookBub Ads they have previously run. I'm guessing Louis de Bernières and/or his publisher hasn't availed themselves of either of these services to date. (For the person who at the back who said, "they probably don't need to…" I heard that, you swine!)

If we click through to Louis de Bernières' page on BookBub, we'll see his covers neatly arranged at the bottom and his slightly bemused profile shot at the top. In-between, just under his bio, is something else I want to draw your attention to: the list of genres he works in. If you then click on Historical Fiction, for example, you will be brought to the genre page on BookBub. There you will see various deals and the like. Ignore their siren call and scroll to the bottom of the page where you will see Recommended Authors—which will probably be led by Ken Follett, unless the world suddenly comes to its senses and starts festooning me with garlands. If you click "View All" you'll get a useful list of potential targets in that genre—very handy for giving you ideas for author targets. Note this for later.

The key takeaway is this: good author targets on BookBub might be very different from those you may have already figured out for Facebook or Amazon Ads. If that doesn't describe you, don't worry, I just want to caution people familiar with those platforms that they can't simply transpose their author targets from elsewhere and expect similar results. This is a common reason why even savvy operators can bounce off BookBub Ads: they import carefully tested author targets from another venue, get frustrated when they don't perform, and write off the entire platform.

Which is an opportunity, if you do it right. We'll go through the process of how you can find your own author targets shortly.

Bidding Basics

Bids are the secret third wheel on the madcap tricycle of BookBub success. Or maybe the secret sidecar of success on the motorbike of BookBub mayhem? I can't decide. Anyway, I made a bold claim earlier about aggressive bidding. Now I need to mine some gold in case y'all cash that check at the same time and collapse the value of DaveCoin.

There are two bidding types on BookBub: CPM and CPC. Most people choose the second, as it's more familiar. This, I shall passionately argue *toute suite*, is a serious mistake.

A CPC ad might save you money on your first amateur spins of the wheel, but a fully optimized CPM ad will beat the pants off a CPC ad any day of the week. Most people don't know this, which is a huge opening for you. That should be enough for you, but I'm not done yet. There's another reason to choose CPM bidding that's worth it all on its own: it teaches you best practices.

For reasons I'll explain momentarily, success with CPM ads is *all* about focusing on CTR, and ensuring it is as high as possible. This makes you a good advertiser, one who burns through audience slower— a crucial factor with the passionate but often more limited audiences on BookBub, at least when compared to the giant ones targetable at Facebook. Focusing on CTR makes you *religious* about testing, ensuring your targeting is rock solid and that your images are on point for those audiences.

It makes you lean and effective, in other words.

While I do occasionally use CPC bidding in very limited circumstances—which I'll delve into—you will invariably get much cheaper costs per click by using CPM... but only if your ads are road-tested first. Only if you show the discipline to test all your comp authors first. Only if you have the patience to nail down your graphics first. By investing that effort, you will get some wonderful results, easily trouncing any CPC campaigns you run.

I'll explain when to bid aggressively and blow the competition out of the water (yet still profit with well-optimized ads). I'll also tell you when you should be more conservative with those bids, when it's smarter to underbid, and even exactly when you could switch to CPC bidding to squeeze the last bit of ROI-positive traffic out of a big campaign. And if you don't know your CPC from your CPM or ROI, and are wondering if I'm A-OK, we'll break it down shortly.

First, we need to look a little more deeply at that great seething mass we have a love/hate relationship with. Other writers!

PART II

ANATOMY OF A KILLER AD

I'm going to spell out what makes a great BookBub Ad, by which I mean one that will generate sales for you. This isn't some wishy-washy "branding" exercise. You will learn what kind of images convert and what targeting options you should adopt to reach the right readers who truly respond to your work. Then I will simplify things a little, explaining why I don't care about bidding so much and how you will be able to keep things cheap anyway, even with that cavalier approach. Once we plow through all *that*, the next sections will guide you through the testing process, and setting up your first campaigns, before circling back to strategy.

4: Attractive Images

I know how writers think; you guys are itching to throw up some ads, and probably want to page ahead to the ninja tricks and killer moves. But no one picks up the nunchucks on their first day in the dojo without hurting themselves; you must have the basics in place. It's fine to want high-converting campaigns, but you can't just skip to that stage—and you'll never get there if you have drab images nobody wants to click on. Let's make sure that's all squared away right from the get-go.

While *you* might fret over targeting and bids and conversion rates, readers only see one thing: a relatively small 300x250 pixel box at the very end of their deals email. *If* they scroll down that far, of course, and if they open their email that day. Many do not! Which means we'd best grab the attention of those who do. Unlike Facebook or Amazon Ads, this image is unaccompanied by text and must do all the work on its own: capturing attention, encapsulating the offer, conveying the genre, and enticing readers to click—the right readers, by signaling the specific niche within.

To be clear, by signaling, I don't mean some form of genteel semaphore. I'm talking highway billboards. Giant flashing neon signs! We're going to be as subtle as a jackhammer, because that's what works.

The design principles behind an effective Book-Bub Ad are not markedly different from that of an effective ebook cover—it should be simple, striking, and clearly communicate the genre to the point that readers *instinctively know* it is the type of book they love. In case it needs to be underlined, this is not a place to be intricate or demure. You have a tiny window—quite literally—to capture attention. The canvas simply isn't large enough to be overly ambitious with your design, or to try an understated approach either, for that matter.

I'll explain exactly what you need in this chapter. Later, I'll tell you how to get it. But even if you hire someone, rather than tackling the design process personally, you still need to know exactly what a great image is comprised of so you can accurately brief your designer. I've done it both ways and can give you pointers for either approach. Unlike designing book covers, the tools today have developed to the point where most people can design serviceable ads for themselves, if they have the requisite patience and time to invest. Otherwise, it's very reasonable to outsource.

What You Need 1: Use Your Cover FFS

This part is straightforward—you need a 300x250 pixel image. That's the only format on BookBub Ads, which makes things nice and simple. But what should that image contain? I've seen a lot of people argue that it's better to have an ad graphic *without* the book's cover, and I believe BookBub may have also recommended this at one point, in some blog post or other.

I firmly disagree. BookBub may have data showing that such ads garner more clicks, but BookBub can't see the most important part of the equation: conversion—something to always keep in mind.

I've done extensive testing across a wide range of genres and the results are very clear indeed: while ads without a book cover *can* generate better CTRs, sometimes, they are always inferior when conversion is factored in—and it's not even close. BookBub Ads with book covers simply convert much better.

I also find the same with Facebook. You could be advertising erotic romance, urban fantasy, or political thriller, and the average quick-scrolling user might not be entirely sure if they are clicking on an ad for a game, or a movie—or a dildo, I guess. It's an easy mistake to make!

That theory doesn't really fly with BookBub, of course, but I think something else might explain this marked conversion discrepancy between ads with and without book covers.

One of Amazon's most successful innovations—and earliest patents—was one-click purchasing. It recognized early on that making the buying process as frictionless as possible greatly increased the chances of buyers completing the transaction. Conversely, anything that gives a customer pause is death. They can have second thoughts, or get distracted by an alternative product or website, or toast popping, or kids screaming, or dogs barking, or the phone ringing, or opportunity knocking on the door with a set of exciting encyclopedias about caterpillar poop and sub-Warholian frescoes.

Any digital marketer will tell you that the worst kind of ad is one that generates a ton of clicks but doesn't convert into actual purchases. It's a seductive kind of failure because it's often *so close* to being a winning ad, but has some key flaws. Usually, the problem is that the ad is making a promise the landing page doesn't keep. I believe—and testing firmly backs this up—that any dissonance between the ad image and what readers see when they get to your Amazon page will make them pause. And if they pause there is a big risk you could lose them to the aforementioned dogs, kids, or delicious slices of buttery, buttery toast—or the 200+ other titles Amazon is now advertising on our book pages. (Seriously, count them.) Or the trillion other sites on the internet. (Maybe take my word on that one.) I mean, there's a whole Tumblr page dedicated to animals that look like Tom Hanks; I'm surprised anything gets done.

Which means I don't just row against the advice to ditch the cover, I often double down and also use the cover art in some way in the background. That said, there are always exceptions. Data trumps the most convincing theories, so feel free to test non-book cover images if you wish and go wild if they actually do convert. Just don't make that your only approach.

What You Need 2: Stress The Damn Offer

The other element your image absolutely needs is a clear and explicit offer. I see people failing with BookBub Ads all the time, and one of the most common reasons—after screwing up the targeting and not having a professional-quality image—is not successfully communicating the offer. This is why I keep stressing that you must remember where your ads appear: right at the bottom of an email containing some fabulous deals from truly household names. If you are trying to palm off a full-price book after all those bargains, you're going to find it a tough sell. This is a deal-hungry crowd—as I will keep repeating, until it sticks.

But what kind of offer? Voluminous testing has confirmed what you might have guessed anyway: the most attractive offer to BookBub subscribers is Free, followed by 99¢. Things get trickier after that—these people expect deals—but sometimes a $1.99 offer can work, or even $2.99. I've even made higher prices work in certain niches where steep discounts are less common. Often though, the most enticing offer you can present here, after free and 99¢, is *new*.

BookBub has historically shied away from promoting new releases to its audience for various reasons. That has changed a little with the advent of New Release Alerts and Pre-Order Alerts and, most recently, New Release Featured Deals. However, I think there is still some latent appetite among its users for information about competitively priced new releases, as the first two services only cater to existing fans of a given author, and the latter service usually contains much higher priced books. In this context, your $2.99/$3.99/$4.99 new release might get some traction. I deliberately say "might"—it can be very hit-and-miss. Really, the best use of BookBub is to promote deep discounts. If you're looking for something to continually push books at higher prices—the El Dorado of book advertising, I guess— then Amazon or Facebook Ads will do a better job of that. BookBub is for *deals*.

While I'm generally loath to disagree with the smart people at BookBub, this is another area where my advice can diverge. BookBub has previously suggested that ads *without* a price perform better, particularly for higher priced books. Once again, I believe this comes from BookBub's less-complete view of the data. They can only see CTR and might naturally assume that performance carries through when it comes to conversion, but my testing suggests otherwise, and once conversion is accounted for, ads *with* a price tag perform much better.

It makes sense too. If an ad has no price, Book-Bub readers may well assume it's free or cheap—a fair assumption in a newsletter specifically for highlighting discounts. And if that ad turns out to be for a higher priced book, they will be surprised (and maybe even feel tricked) when they get to Amazon; customers usually don't complete the transaction in such circumstances. BookBub doesn't see that abandoned shopping cart, just that the reader grabbed one.

As for those ads for free or 99¢ books, I strongly believe you should include the price here also. Free or 99¢ is such a powerful hook that not leading with it is surely missing a trick. I think there are other benefits too. For instance, when I advised using the book cover and the cover art in your ad image, as that matches what readers see when they click through, I think being up front about the price means readers will hesitate less when they get to your page on Amazon. It just makes it all more frictionless, which is definitely what you want. And testing strongly backs up just how seductive a frictionless process can be. (P.S. I was going to use a lube metaphor there but restrained myself. You're welcome!)

Now that you have your book cover and your offer, all you need is some background. The advice here is simple: in most cases, the cover art for your book is the most ideal background of all. Yet again, this comes back to branding, and having no dissonance between what a prospective reader sees in your ad and what they are confronted with on your Amazon page.

Ebooks aren't exactly the ideal medium to show a string of examples which embody these principles, so please check out the BookBub Resources page on my website—*bit.ly/BookBub4*—where I pulled together a bunch of useful things for the readers of *BookBub Ads Expert*, including examples of lots and lots of ads I like, covering all sorts of genres.

5: Discrete Targeting

The most enticing image in the world is completely useless if it's pointing at the wrong people. Targeting on BookBub is quite straightforward, but that doesn't mean it's without pitfalls. Getting this right is so important; it's one of only two primary factors that will determine whether your ads work.

While there are, in fact, four ways to target on BookBub, we will primarily concern ourselves here with author targeting, as this is where most people trip up. It all comes back to the inherent quirks in the system, which means a popular author at a retailer like Amazon may not have many followers on BookBub itself. In turn, this often means a solid-gold comp author—someone you absolutely share an audience with—may not actually be a good target for you on BookBub.

Targeting by author will take up most of our attention for several such reasons, but there are four distinct targeting options on BookBub. You can target by:

1. Retailer;
2. Territory;
3. Genre;
4. Author.

Let me explain briefly why you can pretty much ignore three of those options—for now, at least. In the testing phase, we will be running ads exclusively to Amazon US, as that's by far the toughest ad venue. This makes it the best place to test an ad. If it survives the Thunderdome that is the US Kindle Store, it will slay everywhere else, because the markets outside of Amazon and America are more deal-starved, and generally respond much better to ads (in relative terms, of course).

Conversely, if you only test at Kobo Canada or Apple UK or Amazon Australia, you are going for the lower hanging fruit and the more responsive audiences there will mask flaws in your ad that the US market will brutally expose. But you want this, so you can optimize your ads enough to work everywhere. In other words, the US Kindle Store is a perfect proving ground. Once we have everything in sync, we'll take the band on tour.

You also don't need to worry about genre targeting so much right now, because I simply recommend always selecting your genre as well. You can *just* target by genre, of course, but this invariably results in being served too broadly—and the ads will be both ineffective *and* expensive, which is quite the gruesome twosome. There is also the option of solely targeting by author, but it's good to always throw the genre in there too, as it both covers you for authors who write in more than one genre, and also handily excises the more... casual fan who may like the author you are targeting on an individual level for whatever reason, but may not be a genuine fan of the genre itself. Those people can drag down your ads—particularly with bigger authors, and definitely with those who are household names, so it's good to exclude them where possible.

After selecting your genre—and it's fine to put in two; the system will seek readers interested in *either* rather than both—then you need to input at least one author target. But who? What does a well targeted ad look like?

The system doesn't give a whole lot of useful information within the ads interface itself. To get a read on which author targets will make good potential subjects, and to decide who you should test first, you need to pop over to the reader side of BookBub— *bit.ly/BookBub3*—which has far more useful information for this part of the process.

A note of warning: BookBub is gradually rolling out changes to its website—on the reader side in particular, which is slowly becoming more of destination for readers with reviews and deals and various social aspects too. This means that, at the time of writing at least, some of you will be seeing the older version of BookBub, and some will see the newer iteration. Authors in Canada and the UK, for example, seem to be getting the older version, whereas Americans should see the more up-to-date version. If you are in the former bracket, hang tight. The more extensive site is coming soon to a computer near you.

For everyone who *does* see the updated version of BookBub—and I believe that will describe the overwhelming majority of the glamorous and discerning folk who will purchase this book—you have lots of handy information at your fingertips to help you assess your potential author targets, and also unearth new ones, if needed. And they may be needed once you begin crossing names off your list.

Of immediate interest is how many followers each of your potential targets has on BookBub. The results may surprise you, because the number of followers any author has is largely a function of how many Featured Deals and Ads they have run previously.

This leads to the surprisingly common scenario where a genuinely popular author can have very few followers on BookBub, either because they have never used BookBub Ads, were never selected for a Featured Deal (this happens every day to *huge* authors—often because they are exclusive to Amazon), or perhaps because their parsimonious publisher elected not to spend on either. If you are in Kindle Unlimited yourself and/or a lot of your comp authors are exclusive to Amazon, then it's quite likely they won't have been selected for Featured Deals, even if they have sold millions of books.

This can lead to some weird anomalies. Raymond E. Feist—whose *Riftwar Cycle* books I devoured in my teens—has relatively few followers for such a genuine giant of the genre. The same is true of Frank Herbert, author of the timeless SF classic *Dune*—such a blockbuster hit that successive big names went through torment trying to get it made, from Ridley Scott to Dino De Laurentiis to Alejandro Jodorowsky (who planned to cast Orson Welles, Salvador Dali, and Mick Jagger), before David Lynch finally wrestled it over the line with an almost-as-hilariously-eclectic list including Patrick Stewart, Max von Sydow, and Sting. While we are indulging in tangents, it's interesting to note that Ridley Scott went off to direct the original *Blade Runner* after failing to get *Dune* off the ground, but now *Dune* is about to get the remake treatment, helmed by Denis Villeneuve, fresh off *Blade Runner 2049*. Anyway, even with this renewed interest, Frank Herbert still languishes with a relatively paltry number of followers.

But it's not just writers whose popularity may have been eclipsed by newer, shinier authors, or even those who have shuffled off this mortal coil. Literary phenomenon Isabelle Allende—someone I'm particularly fond of for this quote: "Erotica is using a feather; pornography is using the whole chicken"—is very much alive and kicking, Despite her wit, and a prodigious output, she has barely any followers at all; presumably they're all intimidated by the long-standing critical and commercial success that has seen her sell seventy million books and be repeatedly mentioned as a potential Nobel Prize winner.

This phenomenon isn't just restricted to tradi-tionally published authors either. UK indie superstar LJ Ross has sold over three million books, yet has a comparatively small number of followers on Book-Bub. In fact, it's quite common for authors who have largely spent their career in Kindle Unlimited not to have received any Featured Deals from BookBub and, thus, have few followers on their platform. I'm not suggesting that such authors are missing a trick—

clearly what they are doing is working very well for them—but what this should serve to show is that the World of BookBub doesn't often map reality particularly well, and is very heavily skewed by how much any given writer has played in their sandpit. Remember this when drawing up your comp authors!

You will probably have to cast a wider net than originally envisaged. This is one of the main areas where people screw up. They simply input their normal list of comp authors and can't understand why the ads perform poorly, or don't serve at all. These preparatory steps might seem a little painstaking, but they're necessary, and totally worth it.

I know some of you are eager to dive in and start running ads and stick two fingers up to Mr. Miyagi over here; I get it. I'm a writer too, remember? I'm well aware of how impatient we all can get when it comes to marketing. Some of you have probably already skipped ahead and started running ads with predictably poor results (he says, to some slightly creeped out people who are now taping over their webcams. Too late!).

If you can exercise some patience, however, and methodically go through these steps, you will build a robust list of comp authors who will get excellent results for you every time and add some serious punch to every promo.

6: CPM Bidding

Authors can engage in a lot of hand-wringing and hair-tugging over bidding, but, honestly, I don't care about it at all. Really! I never spend more than a moment thinking about it. And I'm more than a little put out that I have to write a whole chapter on the topic. I blame you guys, quite frankly, and it has been noted in your records.

People generally labor under the false assumption that bidding is the key lever for controlling their costs, but I want to show you another way. A *better* way. One that will make your ads stronger and your costs cheaper. A genuine win-win. And it will also make your life simpler in the long run too, as you won't have to care about bidding either, once you adopt this mindset.

You in? Let's rewind.

BookBub is surprisingly flexible and has two bidding options: CPC Bidding and CPM Bidding. The first will be familiar to most of you: Cost Per Click. Whereas the second might require explanation: Cost

Per Mille—i.e. the cost per 1,000 impressions. And, yes, that's Latin for the non-necrolinguists in the audience.

Having a choice is a relatively new development, because when BookBub Ads first launched, the only option was CPM Bidding. This caused a lot of anxiety, as the concept was less familiar to people. There's also something inherently more reassuring about CPC Bidding, for advertising novices especially. Even for older hands, CPC Bidding can act as an effective brake on costs; you're essentially putting a hard cap on things by saying something like, "I won't pay more than 42¢ a click." And that specific number you decide to bid is presumably based on some kind of return on investment (ROI) calculation.

It's also easier for authors to make those ROI calculations with CPC Bidding. You might have a good idea of conversion rates—one out of six people you deliver to your book's page on Amazon might purchase, to give a simple example—and use that to determine your bid. Or you might get more advanced with such calculations, factoring in things like sell-through to subsequent books in the series. Alternatively, you might just go by gut, and have a rough sense that once bids start to creep north of 60¢ (to give a random example again), ROI is getting problematic for you. All approaches are valid, by the way; some of the smartest operators work more instinctively.

The point is this: CPC is simply easier to figure out and less alien to most authors, so they instinctively gravitate towards it.

When BookBub Ads launched, and only had CPM Bidding, there was much grumbling—from myself included. If you're already on my soon-to-be-world-famous mailing list, with its weekly marketing nuggets of deliciousness, you would have already heard the story of how I was *haranguing* the good folk at BookBub to give us a CPC bidding option. However, as soon as it launched, and I rolled out my first test campaigns, I went running back into the arms of CPM Bidding, swearing fealty until the end of days. Why?

If your ads are fully optimized, CPM Bidding wins every time. (Almost...)

That's a pretty bold statement, and quite a bald one too. But after spending large sums on big BookBub campaigns for some bestselling authors, I'm more confident than ever in making it. There are some teeny tiny exceptions, which means I must (grudgingly) append that minor qualification. But, as a general rule, CPM Bidding beats the pants off CPC Bidding. Because your ads will:

(a) serve more;
(b) cost less;
(c) scale better; and
(d) stretch out your audience for longer.

And if all that wasn't enough, CPM Bidding will also teach you best practices and force you to be a better advertiser.

Those are some big claims, so let me back them up. And when I'm done, you'll be a convert to CPM Bidding too. Prepare thyself.

Let me stress that I say this *despite knowing full well how much easier CPC is to compute*. Don't let the initial difficulty curve put you off. I know that CPC is familiar, and you can calculate it on the fly. CPM, on the other hand, is much more inscrutable. "What does it even stand for? Is that Latin? I don't want to pay for impressions, I want to pay for results." These are objections I commonly hear when recommending CPM Bidding. People saying this have a point! CPM Bidding is not as straightforward. It most certainly is harder to figure out.

More importantly, CPM Bidding is *riskier*.

Much riskier if your ads are bad, and they invariably will be at the start. You don't have a hard cap on what you're paying for clicks—meaning you could, in theory, fly through your budget with little to show for it, because ads with CPM Bidding will generally serve much faster.

So why do I recommend it? Is it just the whiff of cordite?

Because a *fully optimized* CPM ad will trounce a CPC ad any day of the week. It will have a better CTR, because it teaches you best practices, forcing you to really nail down your targeting and images. This makes you a better advertiser, which improves the performance of all your ads, and increasingly so over time. CPM ads will have a lower average CPC because of that better CTR. It will also burn through audience more slowly because of that better CTR— meaning your campaigns won't just be more effective, they will scale better and run for longer too.

That's quite a mouthful, one which probably requires some explanation. Let's take a closer look.

With CPC Bidding, you only pay for results, i.e. if someone actually clicks on your ad. CPM Bidding is different, you pay regardless of whether someone clicks or not. You make a bid—for simplicity's sake let's call it $10—based on what you are willing to pay per 1,000 impressions.

"How is that better?" you might ask, with some justification. Well, it isn't always better. If you have a bad ad that doesn't get clicked on so much, you will definitely be better off going with CPC ads. You will get bad results, not many people will click on your ad, and it might not serve that much either—but at least you won't be out real money. Which is something, I guess.

But if your ad *is* good, and you get lots and lots of clicks—and I will teach you how to do that!—then CPM ads work out to be *much* more cost-effective. You will get far more clicks for your $10 than you would under CPC. It's much more economical. It reduces your costs, which greatly increases your ROI. Which is great!

And that's not the only advantage. It also increases your serving, which is crucial for launches, Countdown Deals, or other limited-time promotions where you have a tight window to maximize sales. CPM ads will give a reliable amount of serving, and you really can depend on it. With CPC ads, the amount of serving can be very spotty indeed, and outside your effective control.

Under CPC ads, it's all about your bid—the only

real factor in deciding whether your ad will show or not. Bid too low, and your ad won't display, as you will lose the auction and someone else will get that ad slot. Hard luck. Try again tomorrow! Bid too high, and your ROI will plummet. You'll be paying far too much to bring those BookBub readers to your Amazon page and losing money overall. Maybe by a huge margin. This is… not optimal.

That balancing act often leads those using CPC bidding to lurch between unprofitable ads and non-serving ads, which is incredibly frustrating, and can also lead you to make some poor decisions about what kind of CPC bid will work for you (out of sheer desperation to get your ads served). This also kills two of the unique advantages of BookBub Ads: reliability and replicability. And that prevents you from scaling effectively too.

Here is the final nail in the CPC coffin: for many desirable author targets, you can't even get your ads to serve at any kind of scale unless you are bidding a dollar or more per click. Which, quite frankly, is crazy. No one should do that. Especially not when you could be paying a fraction of that by doing things another way.

With *optimized* CPM ads, BookBub becomes like a faucet. I can turn it on, sales will gush out in a gloriously predictable manner, and then I can turn it off again, as business needs and budget allow. After running lots and lots of huge BookBub campaigns that helped launch successive books into the Top 100, with immediately profitable ads, I know exactly what I'm going to get from a BookBub campaign at this point. *If* the ads are optimized.

I keep stressing that the ads need to be optimized because success with CPM ads is all about CTR. You must focus relentlessly on improving CTR as much as possible. The higher that number, the lower your effective CPC will be. A simple example will illustrate (don't worry though, BookBub automatically calculates all this for you!):

Scenario 1: *If you are bidding $10 CPM and get a paltry 6 clicks on your ad out of a thousand impressions, you will have a CTR of 0.6% (clicks ÷ impressions = CTR). A low CTR like this will mean a very high CPC. In this particular example, your CPC works out at $1.66, which is waaaaaay too much.*

Scenario 2: *But if you get 14 clicks on your ad, you will have a moderately better CTR of 1.4%. A middling result like this will still lead to a higher than desired CPC, though. Here your CPC works out at $0.71—still too much.*

Scenario 3: *However, if you manage a much more desirable (and doable!) 48 clicks on your ad, that will have a stellar CTR of 4.8%. A great result like this will deliver a CPC you can really work with. In this case, it's $0.21. You can take that to the bank (i.e. turn up the ads and enjoy the ride!).*

The last example, obviously, is a fully optimized ad. There is no way you will ever get a CPC ad to turn in a result like that, not at any scale. Whereas I've run campaigns with 30,000 impressions where that kind of performance held up all the way until the tail-end of the promo. (We're talking hundreds and hundreds of sales from just one campaign on Amazon US alone, in just two days.)

How do you ensure your CPM ads are fully optimized? Testing, testing, and more testing. Your targeting must be spot on; there's no room for error. Later on, I'll go through how you can generate a set of author targets for testing, but that will be just a *potential* list. You will have to test them rigorously to ensure that they're solid-gold comp authors for you. On the plus side, you only have to do that once and the comps shouldn't change from campaign to campaign (unless you write in different niches—in which case you may need a separate set of author comps for each niche, but you probably know that already, from advertising elsewhere).

Images often change from one campaign to the next, however, so these will require some (very quick) re-testing each time. That said, you will probably stumble across some form of "template" during the testing process, or over successive campaigns, and will be able to generate new images quite quickly with some experience—just changing up the offer, book cover, tag line, or background image, where appropriate.

Marginal improvements on the image front can have a radical effect on CTR, which will in turn drive down your CPC and make your campaigns significantly more profitable. When I'm running a big campaign with a lot of budget at stake, I like to play a little game with myself. I make the best possible ad I can, and then step away for a moment and do something else. Then I return and try one more iteration of that ad. I can invariably improve it. (I do this with my blurbs also.)

Some of you may be tempted to skimp on the initial author testing. Don't. You need to have a good group of comp authors you can truly rely on. It might take you some time to get to that point! That's fine; better to take this slowly than to have a middling set of comp authors, because BookBub can be an unforgiving ad platform—he warns once more, while counting his scars—with a very fine line between success and failure.

In case you are also side-eyeing my arguments against CPC Bidding, let me give you one extra reason to be cautious: BookBub recently began serving ads on the website as well as by email but it's only including CPC Bidding ads. While I'm confident they will ultimately get the website placement to work, at the moment the execution is a little patchy. For all sorts of reasons, display ads on websites like this perform worse than email-based ads. While BookBub does break out the data for each placement, the placement itself is *non-optional* for anyone using CPC Bidding, which seems a pretty strong argument to avoid CPC Bidding until they get the website-based ads working properly. At the time of writing, I'm also seeing issues with both the targeting and the frequency with which ads are being shown—another reason to avoid CPC Bidding until this placement is optional (or those issues get conclusively resolved).

In short, the only way to avoid being served on the website, which I recommend for the moment, is to use CPM Bidding.

To recap, these are the three elements that make up a great BookBub Ad:

- attractive images—which are simple and striking and clearly communicate both the offer and the niche;
- discrete targeting—a set of reliable author comps which has been specifically generated for, and tested on, the BookBub platform; and,
- CPM Bidding—which beats CPC Bidding hands down if your ads are fully optimized. It's not even close, people.

Now that you understand what makes a great BookBub Ad, let's put that theory into practice and learn how to build one for yourself.

PART III

TEST PREP

You might picture the Testmobile as a pimped-out camper van with rad machines bleeping and blopping, and some kind of stock price ticker rattling out Data Points, however the reality is often more prosaic: a laptop. But with this humble device you can conquer the world! Or your genre anyway. Before we get you measured for a tiara, we have some tests to run. Which means we need to prep like it's the night before finals. Grab some coffee. You're going to learn how to create images that sell, where to find your comp authors, and what bids you need to succeed.

7: Creating Clickworthy Images

Here's where we get right into it, the fluffers have been handed their cards and it's time for the main course. We're going to take each of these elements—targeting, images, bids—and drill right down until you can make successful ads in your sleep. And we'll spend significant time with each element, so you know each intimately. Then we'll walk you through ad creation, before zooming back and looking at strategy in greater depth, showing you how to make BookBub Ads part of an overall marketing plan *and* when to deploy them for maximum effect. (That's the money-rain part, spoiler lovers…)

We've previously looked at what makes an enticing and effective image. By way of reminder, your book's cover—with appropriate/matching background art—and a clear offer are the two key ingredients. Don't be afraid to take what some might consider a cruder approach. This is a price-sensitive crowd, the image you're playing with is quite small, and the ad needs to grab attention from the typical fast-scrolling, glazed-eye reader. Remember to make sure it stands out and clearly communicates not just your genre, but the respective niche within. For more visual cues, check the BookBub Resources page on my website—*bit.ly/BookBub4*—some tools and information I put together for purchasers of this book.

Now that you're reminded of what you need, let's look at how to get it—either by outsourcing, or by rolling up those notional sleeves of yours. Just don't skip over the process of figuring out suitable images for your particular target audience; even if you're outsourcing, you need to have some understanding of what a good ad should look like, so you can brief your designer accordingly... and get tweaks made if required. Even great designers can miss the mark without the right prompts.

How To Get It—Hiring A Pro

There is a really simple option here—using the inbuilt image generator BookBub provides in the ad creation interface. It's also a pretty bad idea. The images it produces are serviceable, I guess, but quite generic-looking. You can do much better than that, and you really should try if you are going to be spending any money on ads. As you will see yourself after running a few successful campaigns, margins are tight and good quality images can really help with CTR.

As such, having a BookBub Ad designed to a professional level is strongly recommended. It will only cost you a small amount and the improvement in CTR and CPC and conversion makes it a no-brainer—the ad's improved performance will cover that minor outlay in short order. That's not your only option though, and might not even be your best option longer-term. Let me explain.

I started out designing my own ads in Canva—a free online graphic design tool I strongly recommend using if you ever want to design any graphics for yourself. However, I'm not a designer and definitely don't have artistic inclinations in that sense (I can't draw a straight line without a ruler), so my first efforts were not very good. I decided to outsource to a couple of different designers who charged $20 or $30 per ad graphic and saw a huge leap in CTR and sales. I've since gone back to designing my own ad graphics in Canva, but that's after lots and lots of practice—which I'll talk about shortly.

There are designers out there who charge more for this kind of ad graphic, and some are worth it, I'm sure, but cheaper options are available. And even at the lower end of the scale, designers will usually bundle a variation or two of whatever ads your order, allowing you to test and see which is most effective. Previously, designers have even thrown in Facebook Ads for me too, as many designs will translate into that format relatively easily, particularly if you follow my suggestions and use minimal text.

However, the best deal of all usually comes from asking your regular designer to bundle ad graphics when ordering your cover. Depending on your relationship with your designer—if you are a repeat customer, perhaps, they may include ad and promotional graphics along with your cover for free, or for a nominal fee. Pilfering a trick from author Ernie Dempsey, consider getting "blank" ads made—i.e. without a specific price tag—so you can insert the deal price as and when you need it, using them for many different campaigns, depending on whether that title is a new release, a Countdown Deal, a freebie, etc.

Recycling FTW.

How To Get It—Doing It Yourself

Let me stress at the outset that not only am I not a designer, I also have no artistic inclinations at all when it comes to something visual, and as I said, can't draw a straight line with a ruler. Yet I can turn out excellent BookBub (and Facebook) ad graphics. How?

Practice. Well, that and a rather magical tool called Canva.

I remember my sister telling me about it. Her exact words were, "this tool is going to put me out of business." I thought that was a little hyperbole at the time—I had yet to succumb to Canva's charms and was reluctant to try it because of the aforementioned complete lack of any artistic skills whatsoever. But you know what? I design all of my ad graphics in-house these days and can spin something up quite quickly too. So much so, that I didn't even need to outsource when running big BookBub and Facebook campaigns for bestselling authors—who were more than happy to splash out for any number of pro-designed graphics. It was just *easier* to throw them together myself. What sorcery is this?

For people who *do* have some level of design skill, or who own and use Photoshop and aren't intimidated by its complexity, or who have already taken the time to use a substitute like GIMP, this probably isn't for you. Try Canva if you like, but you've probably solved this problem for yourself already. You can simply play around with the above-mentioned elements that make an effective ad until you get something you're happy with—enough to test, at least. But do check out some of the resources below, which may help expedite that process a little.

As for everyone else, which I suspect is most of you, I think investing a little time to learn tool like Canva will keep paying out over the years. Even if you end up outsourcing this job—either initially or permanently—it's handy to be able to make a quick tweak to something that was designed for you, or spin up a quick promotional graphic when you have a sale or a launch.

Remember to check the BookBub Resources page on my website—*bit.ly/BookBub4*—for some help with this aspect. If you *do* get frustrated with Canva and decide to outsource, try it again further down the line, after you've seen a few graphics your designer has produced, and perhaps have another stab at it.

Taking Ernie Dempsey's idea one step further, consider asking your designer to provide you with the separate building blocks of an ad—by that I mean the 3D book cover, the background, some price tags and buttons, so you can just assemble whatever ad you need in the future for each book or series. Dragging and dropping in Canva is something anyone will be able to do right from the start; it's a great way to take your first steps in learning how to do it yourself.

That's exactly the path I followed, and now I can

knock up great promo graphics in no time! It's such a handy skill for anyone to have in these precious last days before the robots take over completely.

8: Generating Potential Author Targets

Top of your To Do list right now is to generate a list of potential author targets. We won't end up testing all of these—many will fall at the first hurdle by not having enough BookBub Followers, or having far too many—so we don't want to skimp on the numbers here. Try to get at least 10 potentials here. 20 is better again! Just don't get too broad—remember that after we winnow this list down, you will be dropping $10 or $15 to test each author separately, so super extensive testing will start to cost you. If your budget is tight, you'll have to tailor some of my advice accordingly. While I firmly believe this is the cheapest way to get good at BookBub Ads, it's not free.

Fair warning: this is a *pain in the ass*. I like it, but I'm weird. Most people do not. I'll assume you are more normal than me, as life generally reinforces this assumption. The good news is that you only have to nail this down once—and maybe re-examine *very* occasionally—and then you are set for umpteen big campaigns.

After concluding this process, you will have a tight group of comp authors that you know get you great results all the time. I call them gold comps. Sometimes I get excited and call them *solid gold comps*, but that's just a flight of fancy. Then you will also have your silver comps—authors you will target during more aggressive promotions, when you are doing a bigger push for whatever reason. They won't get you quite the same level of results, but will be valuable targets nonetheless. And then you could theoretically have a set of bronze comps too, but, really, experience tells me that you if you are reaching for those dudes, it's time to put Mr. BookBub away and play with one of your other toys. You might hear other authors talking about tier one, tier two, and tier three comps. It's the same concept, just worded slightly differently.

Some of the foregoing might seem a little counter-intuitive but keep in mind that BookBub is like the Galapagos Islands of ad platforms. Things can be a little... different there. Normal rules don't necessarily apply, and you will have to grapple with the authorial equivalent of flightless cormorants and blue-footed boobies. You need to generate a platform-specific list of authors you can effectively target on BookBub. But how do you do that? Through testing. *Smart* testing.

Here's exactly how:

1. Get a sheet of paper. I guess a virtual sheet of paper will do in a pinch.

2. Write down a handful of comp authors off the top of your head. Very important note: these aren't authors you write like, but those you *share an audience with*. This distinction is crucial. Often you can share an audience with writers of a very different style, and thinking solely in terms of style or voice can lead us astray here.

3. Add any authors that crop up in the Also Boughts for your books. Also Boughts aren't always a reflection of true organic reader sentiment, so feel free to exclude anyone who doesn't fit. Sometimes a permafree can skew your Also Boughts, or any other kind of book that's pushed to a very broad audience for whatever reason. Also, successful books can be the target of lots and lots of Amazon Ads, which can skew your Also Boughts further. Also Boughts are a really great source of comp authors but keep all this in mind when encountering red herrings.

4. Also add any authors who appear in the Also Boughts on your Amazon Author Page. These tend to be even-better quality targets than those on individual books as they are an aggregated Also Boughts, essentially—less prone to shifting sands, fickle feelings, the vicissitudes of time, and similarly capricious phenomena. Unless you are a multi-genre author, in which case, skip this step.

5. Feel free to throw in any authors that you know give you great results on other platforms such as Facebook or Amazon Ads. At this point, you might be getting worried about the number of names on the list. Don't worry; we're about to trim it down considerably.

6. (Optional step.) Multi-genre authors: I'm afraid you will have to do this for each niche you write in. Cross-genre, multi-series authors: stop sniggering at the back; you guys also. If you have two series with different target audiences for whatever reason, you simply must go through this process twice. You're risking mediocrity otherwise, and you're better than that, damn it.

7. Check the number of BookBub Followers for each author on your list and write it down beside each authors name.

8. Copy that list and keep the original somewhere safe. We're going to start crossing people off, but there are other possible uses for anyone we exclude at this juncture. They could make good author targets for you on other platforms, or potential partners for email swaps or other cross-promo—and could even develop into good future targets on BookBub itself, if they grow their followers or BookBub gives us better ways to target those trad whales.

9. Cross off anyone with more than 20,000 Followers. Yes, that excludes lots and lots of giant authors, possibly even ones who are very juicy targets on Facebook or Amazon. They simply don't work on BookBub—at least I've never been able to get giant trad authors to return any kind of reasonable CTR. If you are absolutely convinced you write like John Grisham and his fans adore your fast-paced legal thrillers any time they are presented with them, then feel free to keep him on your list. Just don't be disappointed when that

test ad targeting Grisham returns a CTR of 0.5% or less, and those clicks are costing you north of $2. (Consider this an advance "told you so," but a super-gentle one!)

10. Similarly, you should eliminate anyone with fewer than 500 followers. Don't actually kill them; just cross their names off your list. This might mean dispensing with some popular Kindle Unlimited authors who are great comp authors for you elsewhere. But if they have a follower count that low, it's mostly pointless targeting them. You *should* be able to find targets with more followers than that. The only exception here is authors of super niche stuff. In those cases, you might have to bundle together lots of authors like this, but that arrangement is far from ideal—with a group, it's hard to determine who is driving your sales and who is costing you money.

11. If you still have a lot of authors left even after The Great Winnowing, then cross off anyone with more than 15,000 followers and fewer than 2,000, which will focus on the sweet spot in terms of follower counts. But if you have a good number for testing already, then we can proceed. To

repeat a warning: just remember you will be testing each of these authors individually, unless they have very low follower counts, and each test will cost you $10-$15. If your budget necessitates going through your list manually and pulling out what you think are the better comp authors to test, then do that at this stage.

You now have a solid list of test authors. But before we can put together our first test ads, we must return to the topic of bids, and give you some specifics to go with my breezy dismissals!

9: Bidding To Be The Boss

I've already convinced you—one sincerely hopes—about the merits of CPM Bidding. No doubt some of you are already eyeing that box where you input bids and wondering if it's *really* necessary to bid as high as BookBub suggests, or whether there are any tactics to extract value from this process, and perhaps if any of that can be applied during the testing phase.

The answers to those questions are yes, yes, and no respectively. Taking them in reverse: we're going to bid high during testing and bully everyone else out of the auction, because we need clean data and we want it now. That said, we will moderate our bidding at least somewhat when outside the Testmobile, and I'll share further tips later for cutting costs. But as a very simple approach to bidding, I suggest going high for testing, medium for the kind of big, blast campaigns that accompany a launch or price discount, and quite a bit lower for the type of drip campaigns that will continually push a permafree or cheap series entry point. You might tweak that approach slightly as you go, and what "medium" or "high" means will definitely vary by genre (and even time of year), but that's a reasonably good rule of thumb.

During testing, though, cutting costs isn't a priority. Establishing solid author comps is, because they will be the real lever with which we will reduce costs, and this will do that job much more effectively than skimping on bids. We need to get to the point of having good author comps as quickly as we can, and we don't want the data muddied by spreading each test over several days. This means we will bid very aggressively at this juncture. In practical terms, this means bidding at the upper end of the range that BookBub suggests *at the very least*. I often add a little to ensure we don't run into the issues that those using CPC Bidding wrestle with every day: sluggish delivery, ads not serving, general ennui. For once, we get to act like billionaires and throw cash around until we get our way!

Before such talk makes you nervous, however, remember what I said: bids aren't really how we reduce costs. Improving CTR will do a *much* better job at that. During testing, we'll bid high, serve fast, analyze results, and then tweak our targeting and images until our ads are fully optimized. Those ads will have improved to the point where CTR is great, which will in turn deliver you a low CPC—significantly lower than anyone running CPC Bidding. (In fact, those guys will struggle getting any serving at all, at CPCs much higher than you will be getting. I'm talking two or three times higher. Fools!)

Let me give a flesh-and-blood example, which will perhaps allay any remaining fears. In a recent round of test ads, I was exploring new potential comp authors and discovered a writer who I seemed to share audience with—enough to consider testing, at least. When creating the ad, BookBub suggested that I bid between $6.56 and $10.00. I pretty much ignored this, because I generally find this range way too conservative—for testing, at least.

I remember a statistician friend saying you can drown in a lake that is, on average, three feet deep. Averages can mask huge variance, is the point, and that's what I believe is happening here. There are many people using BookBub for drip campaigns, which slowly feed readers into a series via a cheap or free Book 1, and a lot of these will be lower budget ads, just dripping away in the background. You can get away with *much* lower bids when you use BookBub in this way. However, that bidding approach will simply not work for a time-limited campaign where you are seeking to make a splash, at scale, over just a few days.

And it definitely won't work for testing. So I go higher—much higher, in fact. I'm happy bidding $12 or more to *ensure* I win that auction. I'm only dropping $10 or $15 on each test, so it's not like I'm going to lose my shirt here. The campaign budget acts as a hard cap to stop things getting out of control (and we'll talk about various ways to do that for proper campaigns later on).

But that doesn't mean I end up paying $12 (or more) for those 1,000 or so impressions I need for my test. The effective CPM—i.e. what you actually get charged—is not the same amount as whatever you bid. All you ultimately get charged is a cent more than the second-place bid, whatever that may be. If James Patterson bids $10 and Harlan Coben bids $12, then Harlan Coben wins the auction—but only pays $10.01—and James Patterson goes home in his Chariot of Nothing.

Returning to my example up top, even though I bid a hefty $12.50 for that author test, I only ended up being charged $9.24.

I only mention effective CPM so you know what it is, and you are less afraid of bidding aggressively. I don't want you to focus on it too much, because CTR is what will reduce your costs, not shaving a few cents (or even as much as a dollar or two) from effective CPM. Focusing on CPM will just lead to incremental gains at best. Focusing on CTR, as I advise, can lead to *giant leaps forward*. Comically outsized leaps. Zero-gravity leaps.

Honestly, I barely even glance at CPM at this point. I don't care if I bid $13 or even more for a test. In my head I have mentally written off $15 to test each author target, and if it comes in much cheaper (which it always does), then great. But I don't sweat it. I want to test each author as quickly as I can and move on to the next, so I can assemble a solid list of targets without too much faffing about. I know $15 will *guarantee* 1,000 impressions quickly, and if I have change from that it's a bonus. Then I move onto the next $15 test—the next author on my list.

You don't necessarily have to bid that high, but I strongly urge you to bid above the range BookBub suggests and ensure you win that auction. As I recommended previously, you will only be running test ads targeting the US Kindle Store in the first instance, as that is—by far—the toughest ad arena, and an ad that survives the cage-fight there should do wonderfully elsewhere. However, it's also the most expensive place to advertise—another reason to bid a little higher in the testing phase. You want that quick, clean, uninterrupted serving, remember?

But be smart too. Deploy tricks like bidding uneven amounts. For example, if you have decided to bid $12.00, then nudge it up to $12.03 or something so you will beat anyone else who has come to the same conclusions. You'll be surprised what a difference that can make.

OK! Now you have all the *ingredients* for your first test ads. Let's build them!

PART IV

OPTIMIZING FOR VICTORY!

You know what makes a great ad, and have assembled all the elements for your own tests. Next, we'll walk through the process, step-by-step, of creating those test ads—and what all the various options on the ad creation interface mean. You will learn how to analyze your results, when a campaign needs tweaking, and how to test your way to fully optimized ads so you're ready for your first real campaigns.

10: Building A Test Campaign

As I walk you through your first test ads, I'm assuming two things: you have professional-quality images and strong bids. Anything less will fudge up the test environment. Initial testing is like nailing down a floorboard. You must pay a little attention to image, then to author targeting, then back to image again—much like hammering one end down a little, and then the other, so nothing gets too out of line. If you are indeed a flooring expert, however, please disregard this hastily assembled metaphor.

Overall, we are seeking to establish which authors work best for you during a small budget test, so you can scale up with confidence. But we also have to check a few image iterations to make sure your ads are as appealing as possible to your target market.

It's generally good practice not to judge an ad before it has 1,000 impressions, which means you could be spending $10-$15 on each test ad. That might not sound like much, but you should have quite a few authors to test, and will probably need to go through several iterations of your image before you are satisfied on that front. Although, sometimes you can snip a really obvious loser before you have reached that level of spend—an ad with just two clicks in the first four hundred impressions is unlikely to have a dramatic turnaround in the next six hundred. Just be conscious of the fact that clicks and impressions are reported by two different systems and often one can appear on your dashboard faster than the other, leading you to think a middling ad is an outrageous success. Or the opposite. It really can go either way.

The testing process will take your whittled-down list of comp authors and show you which will be the most profitable. You will also begin to get a handle on the type of images (and image elements) your target audience best responds to. I have given you some shortcuts in that regard already by telling what audiences *generally* respond to.

That advice wasn't just pulled from the ether; it's based on analyzing results from hundreds of thousands of ad impressions, hugely successful campaigns I ran for several authors across multiple genres. It's also based on comparing results and insights with dozens more writers working in every imaginable commercial niche. However, as it with everything when it comes to book marketing, there are elements of genre variance. The last bit of legwork must be done by you—your particular list of comp authors is unique to you and your books.

Indeed, you may write in a couple of different niches in the same genre yourself—for example, one series might fall squarely under the Thriller label whereas another might be more comfortably shelved under Crime or Action/Adventure. You may well have a different set of comp authors for each series. And it's entirely possible you'll discover that each separate target audience responds better to a slightly different visual style. As I've said before, little differences can lead to big improvements with BookBub Ads.

What we'll do now is go through all the options available when creating an ad—which will also serve as a handy refresher—and then we'll speak about improving those invariably mediocre results until you are happy and getting lots of cheap clicks.

One last thing. You might have your images and author candidates all lined up and ready to go, but which book of yours should you use here? I generally prefer testing on a 99¢ book, and aim to get CTRs of 2% or better, but you can use a freebie or a $1.99 deal if you prefer. Just remember to adjust CTR expectations accordingly.

Okay! Now that the appropriate caveats have been

scarfed down like perfect little *vol au vents* arranged just-so on a plate… where was I? Yes: testing. Now, this chapter would be a lot more digestible with accompanying screenshots, is what you might start thinking, as you go through this. And you would be right. Because I don't want to leave you hanging, I've reproduced this step-by-step guide on the BookBub Resources page on my website—*bit.ly/BookBub4*—filled with all sorts of handy things for readers of this book, so you can peruse it while creating your test ads at your computer, if you need that pictorial assist.

For those who haven't immediately run off to experience these instructions in glorious Technicolor, then let's see if mere words can do all the work!

I'm going to walk you through ad creation; just keep in mind that you are now in the testing phase and we do things a teeny bit differently. First, you are only going to target Amazon US. It's absolutely the case that clicks can be cheaper elsewhere, but Amazon US is the best place to test your targeting for reasons already elaborated upon in depth previously. Just remember that if you have a winning ad on Amazon US, you can roll it out elsewhere with great confidence. If you can make it there, you'll make it aaaaaaanywhere.

Ahem.

I'll quickly run through ad setup and point out anything important. Assuming you already have a BookBub Partners account (if not, set one up as soon as possible), log in, click on the Ads tab from the navbar at the top of the screen, and then select the green button in the top-right of the interface marked Create New Ad. Note that I have used the same headlines for each step below as should appear on your BookBub Ads interface for ease of reference. You can thank me via statues.

Step 1: Choose A Book (Optional)

This *should* be obvious, but sometimes the system misses your book. Add it here if you can, but if you still can't select it—even after adding your book—don't worry. I find this to be a little glitchy at times, but it doesn't ultimately matter. The only function this serves, aside from tracking some data for you to analyze later (which you can do manually) is to auto-populate the links for your ad, which you can do manually yourself. It's wise to add your book anyway if it's not already on BookBub, but don't worry about this otherwise.

To be absolutely clear: there is zero effect on the performance of your ads and this step can be comfortably skipped.

Step 2: Ad Creative

You should already have a pro graphic to drop in here in the section named Upload Existing Creative (or you will shortly). Whatever you do, don't use BookBub's tool here to build your image—which appears when you click Build New Creative, if you are curious. While this tool doesn't do a bad job *per se*, you can do a lot better than that yourself—and little differences can be crucial on this platform. Don't get lazy here! Put in the effort to make your image amazing, and you will reap the rewards in terms of improved CTR, lower CPC, and better conversion.

Step 3: Click-through Links

If you associated a book with your ad in Step 1, you will see that one or more links have auto-populated in this section. We will be restricting ourselves to Amazon US for the purposes of these tests, so remove any others the system has inserted by clicking the on/off button to the left of the link. However, if you didn't associate a book with your ad in Step 1, then simply insert the link manually yourself in the indicated spot. The system will automatically recognize which retailer and territory it relates to using cyber-sorcery.

Whether your link was inserted by the system or by you, triple-check that link. As in, actually click on it, don't just glance at it. This is a great habit to get into, by the way. While mistakes are rare—and usually on the user side, to be honest—getting this right is important enough to devote a whole click into checking whether your ad is pointing at the right place. From personal experience, mistakes are most likely when your eyes glaze over after doing lots of test ads, or complicated campaigns pointing at different places. Be especially careful in those situations.

There also a known bug involving links you've switched off at this stage turning back on again on the confirmation page—but I'll return to that when we get to that confirmation screen, as you can't do anything about it right now. Consider the problem flagged, yo.

Step 4: Audience Targeting

As you already have your possible author comps from the process outlined earlier, the only wrangling here is deciding how many to lump together. Obviously, you will get the cleanest read from testing one author at a time, but some of your potential comp authors might only have 500 or 1000 BookBub followers. In such cases, throw a few similar authors together. Aim for a total of a few thousand followers to get enough serves (you are shooting for at least 1,000 impressions here). Keep in mind that some of those following a given author will be based outside of America or shop somewhere other than Amazon; others won't open their email that particular day. It varies quite a lot.

This sounds a little hazy. But don't worry; there is a handy visual indicator in the form of a colored dial beside the Book Category field. Don't aim for the yellow zone on the right—that's an indication your targeting is too broad. You really want it up the middle, with the system saying "Defined," ideally. If you are in the red zone, that means your audience is too narrow for the ad to serve and you need to add more authors. And possibly coffee.

Just make sure to also filter by genre ("Refine by Book Category" in the parlance of the interface). Remember, many authors write in more than one genre, and it's important to narrow your audience, or your CTR will drop. BookBub is a platform where small margins can make a very big difference, which I will repeat until this mantra is tattooed on your brain by a drumming of woodpeckers, which I'm reliably informed is actually the respective collective noun.

Step 5: Schedule & Budget

It doesn't really matter which dates you pick, as you will be pushing to serve the ad as soon as possible, but it's always wise to put an end date in of tomorrow or some such. Without wanting to pack you all off to the nunnery, this is another good habit to get into. While it hasn't happened to me on BookBub, I have started an experimental test campaign on Facebook without putting in an end date, then promptly fell sick for a few weeks, and then wept uncontrollably when seeing what my card was charged at the end of the month—with very little to show for it in terms of sales. I can't even bring myself to type the amount; I may need sustained therapy before I'm able to take that step. Or perhaps my old friend Mr. Whiskey could take care of those brain cells for me, and we'll call it even.

As for the budget, just drop in $10 or $15. You might not spend all of it, and you definitely don't need to spend more—that will get you around 1,000 impressions, which is more than enough to know whether an ad will work. Select the option to "Fulfill as quickly as possible" as you don't want to spread out the serving and drag out the testing process; you want results now. (Although I often choose this option even when not in the testing phase, as I prefer to micro-manage the budget—more on that later.)

Step 6: Bid

We are testing, and we want results quickly. This means bidding aggressively and bullying everyone else out of the auction. You might bid a little more competitively in the future (a lot more competitively if you are doing a drip campaign on a permafree, for example), but now is not the time for niceties—there is precious data to be harvested.

Choose CPM ads, as they will serve quickest and most reliably, and will also keep your test ads away from the BookBub website, where you definitely don't want them as the CTR will plummet—and CTR is the metric with which will determine the relative strength of a comp author.

Enter a bid that easily exceeds the higher end of the range BookBub is suggesting for your genre/author targets (i.e. $12 or $13 – it varies based on demand and targeting).

Check Your Work

All that's left on this ad creation screen is to name your ad—e.g. "Get Rich Quick Scheme #5186"—and hit continue. You'll then come to a new screen where you will review all your information before your ad goes live, and you should absolutely do that: check your image, targeting, links, the lot. Sometimes you make a mistake, but sometimes the system switches back on a link to Amazon UK or Apple Australia that you had previously switched off. Other bugs have popped up previously—like the image associated with the ad disappearing. In short, if something looks funny on this confirmation screen, don't ignore it. Usually this is a sign that something has gone awry. Simply click the button below to go back and fix it. Make sure to thoroughly check everything at this point because the ad will serve very quickly and spend your money just as fast too.

That's it! Now pour yourself a stiff one as we go over those results and figure out how to make some improvements.

11: Evaluating Results

Yikes. What did you do? I hope you wore gloves because this is a goddamn crime scene.

I don't need to be the reincarnated ghost of St. Polycarp of Smyrna—for the non-Catholics in the audience, that's the patron saint of earaches and prognostication—to guess that your first tests did not post record CTRs. Coffee might be for closers, but ice cream is for sulkers, so dig in. When you're done, we'll cast a beady eye over those initial results and try to identify where things went wrong.

If you know what split-testing is, how to do it, and have a firm grasp on the importance of granular targeting in digital advertising generally, then feel free to skim this chapter. For the rest of you: strap yourself in for the ride of a lifetime! Okay, okay, perhaps it's not that exciting. But it will make you smarter with ads, which will make you more money, and that can be used to purchase bungee jumps, pecan pie, threesomes, or bottles of Mezcal.

Data is everything to modern day marketers,

especially those flogging digital products; once ads show a positive ROI, they can simply turn up the juice and count the number of ducats flowing in. Where they earn their salt is in that first step: putting together a profitable ad. The path to that point generally involves testing—split-testing in particular.

Split-testing is a very simple and effective approach. It involves running two ads that are almost identical but just have one variable different and comparing results between them. For example, let's pretend one ad is targeting Nora Roberts, and a second is aimed at followers of Debbie Macomber. Everything else about the ads, i.e. the image and bid and so on, is identical because we just want to isolate one element—the author targeting—and see which performs better. In this theoretical test, I might get 0.8% CTR on the Nora Roberts ad and 2.2% CTR with Debbie Macomber, which clearly shows I'll have more joy targeting Debbie Macomber's followers.

While that 2.2% CTR is quite good, it's not spectacular, and I might seek further improvements by testing an alternative image. To get the cleanest results, we should only change one element at a time. In this case, I would need to run another test ad to Debbie Macomber's audience, to see if the alternate image performs better with them.

In the last chapter, I said you must pay a little attention to image, then to author targeting, then back to image again. In truth, you should focus a little more on the author element at the start of the testing process, and switch to predominantly testing image variations towards the end. I find it better to get a handle on which authors are going to be real candidates for me first, before iterating the image. Otherwise, I could waste a chunk of money testing five different images on an author who turns out to be a dud with *any* image. And some of your author targets will surprise you at an early stage by getting abysmal CTRs. (Don't worry; others will make it up to you by being surprisingly good targets! It's just another reason never to make any assumptions with BookBub Ads.)

You may wish to work through your list of potential comp authors first before trying out different images. If you get a solid winner—or something close to it—from this initial round of testing, you can then take that author and try a few image variations to see what works best. And if the improvements are significant enough, you may wish to revisit some of those initial failures, or you may have more authors to try out instead.

The margins between success and failure on

BookBub can be surprisingly thin, and the smallest change in an ad can lead to a massive improvement in CTR—turning an ad from a clear loser into an obvious winner. Swapping out a tagline in your image for some social proof (review quotes, author quotes, sales numbers, review numbers, awards, bestseller status, etc.), is definitely worth testing. Or vice versa. As are different colors, position of any button, price tag (and particularly the size/attractiveness thereof), background art, contrast, and so on.

There's always something else you can fiddle with, and CTR is generally a superb guide as to how readers are responding to your ads. Sometimes you can test various elements with little improvement, and then one small change leads to a huge leap in CTR, which in turn pushes your CPC down considerably. Keep at it. It's crucial to narrow things down in this manner—that's the bedrock for success in digital advertising. BookBub has an audience of millions and millions of people. You need to filter out the broad swathe of those who have little interest in your work, or your ads won't work.

Okay, that's the theory. Now go practice.

You still here? Damn it, my editor was supposed to take out the snippy scissors when I gave the secret code word back there. And now I have to present an episode of Beyond The Fourth Wall without so much as a script.

If you got tepid results on your first tests, console yourself in the knowledge that this is a process, not a light switch. And you have already skipped a few steps by reading this book (its author says, with two Xanax overriding his usual urge to be humble). The key thing to remember at this point is that CTR can vary wildly—and that also goes for the most well written, commercial novels from the very biggest authors. Even if you are a word wrangler *par excellence* and a preternaturally talented ad maven, you can easily struggle with your first test ads (and wonder if I'm full of crap).

Which I am, but about *other things*. Don't buy my book on trouser ferrets, is what I'm saying.

Your first test ads might have delivered a stinky result like 0.24%. Suddenly the gap between that and the nominal target of 2% seems unbridgeable, but you will need to improve further still. If you want to scale these ads, you don't want the campaign starting out on the threshold of profitability. You need a little more wiggle room if you are going to serve this ad to thousands more people and keep it in the black.

In theory, the exact CTR percentage that works

for you will vary, as the exact CPC that ad results in will also vary too, and the rate at which that CPC declines over time is not exactly predictable. But nobody's here for moldy old theory! In practice, I prefer to see 3%+ CTR on 99¢ deals. That gives me confidence that I can scale the ad and still deliver sub-50¢ clicks.

If you get that with your first test ads, great. But if you didn't—and I'm going to go out on a limb of the biggest Sequoia tree in the world here and guess that includes nearly everyone—then read on.

Help is at hand.

12: Tweakers of the World Unite

Welcome aboard the Optimization Express! Your first stop is… despair. I recommend moving to the carriage at the rear of the train, which contains the well-stocked bar. And while you enjoy your complimentary chloroform juice, let me commence an extended anecdote.

There are a lot of things I advocate rushing—choosing menu items at a group dinner, marriage, barricades of any kind—but the testing stage is not one of them. I'll level with you: I thought this was all bullshit. I was testing the Living Jesus out of everything and barely scraping 1% CTR on my sexiest targets and wondering what the fuss was about. How could people say that BookBub Ads were working for them? No matter what I tried, I couldn't make a good ad, and was beginning to suspect the good intentions of anyone who told me it was possible.

I'd love to be able to say it was *one simple trick* that set me on the right road at last, but it was a painful and laborious process. And expensive. One which can't be summed up in a simple takeaway.

Sucks to be you!

How To Optimize BookBub Ads

As Stalin once said, you can't make an omelet without committing genocide. So get ready to commit mass murder! Of your design darlings, that is.

I make several images for each campaign. Even with author sets that deliver excellent results every time, and audiences where I've more or less developed a template for images—as in, I place the book in the same place every time, have the same button, tagline, price tag, whatever, as well as a certain color palette for that series or niche—I still develop a couple of alternate images before testing the first that I was happy with. Naturally, I'll have a favorite out of the two or three or four images that come out of that process.

And guess what? My favorite rarely wins. Sometimes none of them do, and it takes one more stab at the image before these audiences—reliable audiences I've used lots to great success, remember—deliver a CTR I'm happy with.

Let's get into specifics a little more—or as much as I can, at least. Obviously, I can't see the quality of the images you are using, the caliber of book you are advertising, for that matter, or how well matched your putative comp authors truly are. But let's assume that stuff is at least *somewhat* there.

If I'm testing a 99¢ book and get a result below 1% CTR, it's unlikely a better image will get that CTR where I need it to be. I usually cross these authors off my list right away. A CTR somewhere between 1% and 2% is usually something you can work with, however. Often, targeting these authors again with an improved image can bring CTR up quite considerably. Not always though, so for now I plonk those authors in the questionable environs of the Maybe Pile.

Anyone netting a 2% CTR or better at this stage automatically enters The Winners Circle. I'll probably be able to improve that CTR even more with those improved images I'll be working on for Team Maybe, but I can relax a little as soon as any test candidate enters this zone, knowing that I'll have at least one workable target for my future campaigns, damn it. Expect that population to grow as you make those image improvements, but don't sweat it if the number of authors you are dismissing, or attaching question marks to, is larger at this point. That's normal. And if you have to go back to the well and gin up new test candidates, I wouldn't stress about that either. Unless you have an unnatural flair for recognizing true comp authors, that's standard too.

What exactly do you improve with those images? You will get better at this with practice, but here's a bunch of questions you can ask yourself if you are staring at your ad graphic and wondering why it didn't generate the hoped-for result:

(a) Is the cover prominent enough? Or did you squeeze it into the corner in an ill-advised attempt to shove in more quotes about how amazing you are? Remember that thing about showing, not telling? Try that here. Ditch the blurb quote (or make it more compact) and embiggen the cover. Let it shine! It will do the selling for you better than any fancy-pants tagline or quote. I usually make it as big as possible, unless there is a very good reason not to.

(b) Is your background a steaming pile of meh? Or is it a scene stealer like Captain Jack Sparrow, staggering on set and bringing a rather milquetoast romance between the supposed leads into sharp focus? You want neither of those things. It should complement your cover, but not distract from it. The reader's eye should be drawn primarily to the cover and the offer (i.e. usually the price-tag). This is one of the trickiest bits to get right, and changing up the background can revolutionize an image. Using a zoomed in part of the cover, or something plainer that repeats some cover elements, usually does the trick.

(c) Is your offer clear enough? Is your price tag prominent enough? Can you make it bigger? Can you make it pop more? Sometimes the needed tweak is that simple and crude. The image is small enough in that email and it has to be kind of shouty to get noticed.

(d) What color scheme are you using on that price tag or button? White text on a red background or black text on yellow background are usually the most effective… even if they clash with the actual colors used in the ad. This is another one of those things where you might have to ignore your Inner Artist and try something cheesier. If it works, it works (and it usually works).

(e) Is there too much text? Is it drawing the eye away from the cover/offer? Is the image too crowded? Some of the most effective ad images I've made have had a price tag and a cover, and little else. The prettiest? Not by any stretch, but very effective indeed. If you have been going text-heavy, try ditching the tagline and see what result you get. The ad might feel… empty, but test it!

(f) Alternatively, your ad might be *too* spare. Some readers place more value on social proof than others, or bestseller status, or a witty tagline. Try drumming up some cred and puffing yourself up a little. I know it doesn't come naturally to most of us, but test it and see how your target audience reacts. Let them decide which ads are best.

You *should* start to see improvements with the above. But if these tweaked images aren't doing anything for you, then you probably took a wrong turn with your set of comp authors and you might need to backtrack. And if *that* isn't the culprit, then try a different designer (especially if that designer was you); perhaps you need a totally fresh visual approach.

This process can test your patience, but you only go through full-on testing once. After that, your comp author list will be pretty much set in stone. You might add the odd author to that group over time as you unearth new comps, but I find the performance to be remarkably consistent with any target that survives the testing process. I've never really had to do any culling.

I should also point out that you can often see a better performance in a real campaign than during testing. Because you are splitting out all your authors into separate tests, where possible, there is a danger of audience overlap and ad fatigue.

Let's imagine I'm an author of paranormal mysteries, and the comp author list I wish to test is a pretty solid line-up containing ten authors squarely in the optimal range of followers—like Angie Fox, Tonya Kappes, Kristen Painter, and Deanna Chase. There is naturally going to be some audience overlap in a tight list of authors like that, meaning that fans of Deanna Chase are also likely to enjoy Kristen Painter, for example.

Anyone following them both on BookBub could easily see my test ads more than I would like if I'm targeting these authors in separate campaigns, as I will be when testing. This drags down the performance as readers won't click more than once, of course. But when I do get around to running those real campaigns, outside of the testing process, I will be combining all my best authors into one big campaign so there will be no audience overlap and I won't suffer the resultant ad fatigue.

Remember, the aim of this testing process is to generate one big group of authors that you will target together on your future campaigns. You won't be splitting them out like you are now—that's purely so you can do proper split-testing, and see who is working and who isn't. Otherwise, we would only be guessing. This author group will be your top-tier BookBub comp authors—your gold set, one you can rely on and will deploy in every campaign.

As I alluded to earlier, I also recommend having a second-tier set; I call them silver comps. These might be some of the Maybe guys that just fell a little short. I'll use them for more aggressive campaigns, ones where immediate ROI is less of a priority—like launching a new series where promotional opportunities are curtailed, perhaps, or a free run in a long series with stellar sell-through, where I *know* I'll make it up on the back end.

We'll talk more about how to run proper campaigns in the next chapter. I just wanted to show you where you're headed so you can get your bearings, and don't get too downhearted if the first results are less than impressive. You might have to test ten authors—and multiple images—before you're anywhere near happy; you could have to test twenty! But you'll get there.

Once you have a solid set of comp authors, you are ready to run your first real campaign. Which means it's time to get deep into strategy. Armchair generals: activate.

PART V

DEPLOYING THE TROPES

Now that you've tested vigorously and have both a key understanding of the elements that make a winning ad *and* how to make one for yourself, we'll look at something just as important: when to use them. Becoming a BookBub Ads Expert isn't just about mad ads, it also requires a keen sense of strategy. Like any tool at your disposal, you'll get the most bang for your buck if it's part of an overall plan. Especially one that *makes it rain*.

13: When To Use BookBub Ads

Your images and author targets have been prodded and tweezed to the point where you are happy to call your ads optimized. The testing process has also familiarized you with the ad interface and you're ready to roll out a campaign to a wider audience. Exciting!

But before you go running off into the night, I want to show you how to *really* use BookBub Ads. We're talking strategy, people. And we'll start basic before getting into some complex stuff, kicking off with the most fundamental question of all: when should you use them?

We could slice and dice this many different ways, but I can simplify it for you: there are two ways of using BookBub Ads: fast and slow. Okay, maybe that's too simple. Let's have another go. There are two ways to use BookBub Ads: in a righteous burst like the machine gun scene at the end of *Scarface*... or spread over an extended period like some kind of sexy sales butter. I'll show you both ways, of course, but let me explain that distinction a little, as it will particularly affect things like bidding and budgets.

If you're in Kindle Unlimited, you probably lean towards burst marketing—i.e. focusing your marketing attention and dollars over a concentrated period, often for things like Kindle Countdown Deals, which will run for a maximum of seven days; free promotions, which only go for five days; and the like. Any ad spend you have might be more focused on these time-limited promotional windows.

But if you opted for wider distribution outside of Amazon, it's quite possible you prefer a slower drip-style approach, where you lean towards having things ticking away in the background, with income coming in at a slower pace but from lots of different sources. And any ad spend in which wide authors engage might be on a lower daily budget, but running constantly—a free or cheap Book 1 getting a constant push, or ads continually running on all series entry-points (back catalog and budget depending).

One approach isn't inherently better than the other, you'll just be using BookBub Ads "fast" or "slow" respectively, which will affect the overall level of serving you will be shooting for, which has a knock-on effect on daily budgets, as well as bids.

The lines aren't that neat, though.

Even if you're wide, you will surely be launching a book or running a sale at some point, where you will be pushing hard over a few days, no doubt augmented by ads. You'll be doing it "fast" and seeking to maximize sales in a limited window. Conversely, even if you are exclusive to Amazon, you may have a lower level of ads running on that background on certain key titles in your catalogue—usually the ones that make the best introduction to the universe of you.

As with "wide" and "exclusive" authors more generally, I think it's smart to be aware of winning strategies of all kinds; even if their application isn't immediately obvious, there will come a time when you need to lean on a different approach.

Doing it Fast

The level to which your ads will be served is dependent on your bids and budgets, but will also be defined by your set of author targets. If you are only targeting one author with a couple of thousand followers, the maximum that ad will be served is far less than if you are targeting several authors with ten thousand followers in the one campaign—the latter potentially delivering hundreds of thousands of impressions and possibly costing thousands of dollars (and generating thousands of sales too, I should note). Those numbers are necessarily vague, you'll notice, because the performance of ads will be entirely dependent on their quality.

If you skimped on testing, your ads might serve a lot but get poor results. This can still cost you significant amounts—even without many clicks—if you have opted for CPM Bidding. And you'll probably only realize how badly the ads performed after all your money is spent. Things move very fast indeed in the world of BookBub.

Some authors start with the best of intentions, but then decide to skip ahead with a partial list of author targets. They might get reasonable results initially, but then they can hit a wall—because their ads have served to everyone the requisite number of times. BookBub will serve an ad to a user up to four times. (This is fine; I'm just noting it, and we'll tease that out in a bit.) The danger in this scenario comes from just throwing ads at new targets, flush with that initial success, without testing them properly. You can test on the fly; I do it all the time. Just remember to limit your spend on untested authors until they properly prove themselves.

Despite spending running lots of big budget campaigns—with astounding results in places—and even though I have battle-tested targets that have proven themselves over and over, as well as enticing image templates nailed down for the respective genres, I *still* drop a $10 or $15 test before rolling out every new campaign, big or small.

I take my proposed ad image, and my "gold" and "silver" author targets, I point that ad at the US Kindle store *only* (no matter where the campaign will ultimately be served), I bid high to bully everyone else out of the slot (at least for this quick test) and then I wait.

That wait is a killer when money is burning a hole in your pocket, and a set of 18-carat gold authors are waiting to kidnap readers for you. But I still do it before *every single campaign*.

Why?

Remember when I said the margins between success and failure were wafer thin? An example should help here. I can roll out a test ad and see a 2.2% CTR—that's pretty good, click costs are in the zone. But I don't just want 1,000 impressions over the whole campaign. I want 10,000 impressions or maybe 20,000 or more. 2.2% doesn't leave a lot of room to scale that campaign up to where I would like, not when you consider that performance will ultimately deteriorate over time (it's not exactly even, and performance can fluctuate, but that's the general trend if you zoom back enough).

Which means I seek improvements in that image before I start the campaign proper. The ad is already pretty good, so I don't want to make wholesale changes here; it only needs a tweak. I might switch up a color or play with the contrast or try and make the text look a little more professional. Maybe I'll make the price tag bigger. Or stress the offer more.

And then I test again.

Invariably, I'll see an improvement. Maybe it will jump to 3.4% or something like that, and then I can turn the juice up with confidence, knowing this one will scale beautifully.

What does that mean in practice? Well, BookBub can spend your money in an instant. I don't think it's a good idea to just assign your budget and ask the system to spread it evenly over your chosen dates. I prefer to micro-manage it and squeeze out a better performance. I find that works far better overall and allows you to be more reactive. Choosing to tell the system to spend your money as quickly as possible is the way to go here, but you have to put manual caps on the overall spend to stop it going out of control.

When scaling up an ad, I might increase the budget to $100 or $150. It's important to note that budgets are cumulative on BookBub. This means if you're turning your last test ad into a proper ad, you just need to add money to the budget on top of whatever has been spent already. If your test budget was $15, and that's been spent, and you want to throw another $100, then increase the budget to $115. Similarly, if you are adding another $50 into the pot later, then increase it to $165. You must keep adding; it doesn't reset unless you actually start a new, separate campaign.

I tend to add money in $50, $100, or $150 increments, depending. That also limits any damage if a campaign starts to deteriorate and CTR plummets. But it's enough of a spend to generate meaningful sales if the ads are running hot too. I'll even micromanage like this for campaigns with overall budgets of several thousand dollars, and suggest you do likewise at any budget outside of what might charitably be described as "optimistic."

After you run a few campaigns of this type, this will all be a little more instinctive for you. You will know, for example, that your "gold" list of authors will burn through around $300 over a day or two until CTR starts to dip. (Note: this is random example, not a rule of thumb.) Perhaps you'll get to a spend of around $500 before CTR really starts to decline and it's time to stop that campaign. Or maybe you'll know that your "silver" set of comp authors is good for around 25,000 impressions before it gets a bit wobbly.

This is a Spidey-sense you will develop (one dependent on your particular author sets). Start cautious. Watch closely for your first few spins of the wheel, until you start to gain that instinct. After that, you can be much more hands off; the babysitting stage can be educational, but you don't want to spend your life doing it.

Once you develop that sense of your own set of comp authors, BookBub becomes very reliable and everything tends to operate within expected parameters. And when you get to this point, it really feels like playing the game of advertising on Easy Mode.

To give a real-world example, I typically run an ad over five days, which gets 25,000 to 30,000 impressions—and that's one of several ads I'll have running overall—with CTRs starting at around 4% on Amazon US, and they're still up around 2% or so when the campaign gets snipped or otherwise peters out. This all leads to excellent CPCs, and top-quality clickers too. Conversion rates of 20% to 25% are usual enough—something you would *kill* for on other platforms.

I want you all to get to this point, and you can.

You may need to go through the testing section (and perhaps the process) a few times. But if you can tough it out, the rewards are immense.

Maybe this approach—burst marketing, I mean—is a little extreme for certain authors and certain books. Perhaps you would be more suited to figuring the system out at a slower place, with lower stakes and a lesser budget. You could be more methodical and risk averse, and less impulsive or aggressive.

That option exists! We can play with drip campaigns, and take it nice and slow.

Doing it Slow

Here's the thing. While all those pumped-up fiends are running around, spending their money like there's no tomorrow, we're going to kick back. Play it cool. Wait for our moment to strike. The others can wave that blunderbuss around as much as they like; we're smarter than that. We are a *goddamn rapier*; we'll strike quickly and precisely and then exit with a minimum of fuss. Welcome to a completely different way to use BookBub Ads. With a burst approach to marketing—like supporting a launch or Countdown Deal—you are seeking to compress attention and sales into a tight window. You're often maximizing reach, rather than profit. You're seeking to scale, rather than whittle away at margins. You want to hit all of your audience as quickly as possible. And you might even go into the red to do it.

Drip marketing is much more strategic. You'll hang back, wait for prices to fall. Then you'll roll out your ads. Metaphorically speaking, of course. You don't have to micro-manage that part—the system will do it for you.

Let's assume you're a hard-working and impossibly glamorous author of romantic comedies. That may not describe all of you but—hey—two out of three ain't bad. You have a six-book series and the first book is at 99¢ permanently now, after being at $2.99 for a while. You're wide, after previously playing in the Kindle Unlimited pool with moderate success, but that's not so important in the first part of this example. Much more relevant is that you aren't in any *particular* rush to move that Book 1 (as long as it happens at some point). That 99¢ deal isn't time-limited; it's a permanent price point. You simply don't have the same time-pressure as a Kindle Unlimited author often does, and you can use this to your advantage.

Specifically, if you need twenty sales—for example—on that Book 1 every day to keep enough fresh meat funneling through the series so your car won't get repossessed, then it will be smart to bid a little lower than those Kindle Unlimited-types looking for a burst of action.

Your effective CPM can drop considerably when you aren't in a hurry.

The exact amount to which you can drive those bids down will totally depend on your daily budget, author set, and a dozen other variables; you might surprise yourself here. Play around with the numbers and try to be patient. See how it pans out over time. And if you have gold and silver author sets, you can try different bids and approaches with each, because the water-mark will be different for each author, and each author set. You can even try super low bids on any bronze (or third-tier) author comps you identified during the testing process and so callously dismissed. Maybe you can low-ball the bids enough that a poor CTR will still deliver clicks at a reasonable price. *Maybe*. That's for later on, though, when you have more experience. Focus on the stronger comps first.

The basic advantage drip marketers need to lean into can be illustrated with a simple example of how the auction often plays out: if I'm a heavy hitter spending $500 a day with a $13 CPM bid (which is very high), I could be bust by 9:00pm, all my money spent—even with that substantial budget. My ads will stop serving at that point, of course, which will lead the necessary bid for ads to get served to drop, because Mr. Big Spender is no longer in the auction, driving up prices. The winner will be the next highest bidder, and that could be someone at a much lower level. You could be lurking in the shadows clutching a sweaty twenty, and might even get a spin with a relatively paltry $6 CPM bid before the dance is over.

BookBub Ads, when used in this manner, become a weird game of Russian Roulette on a twenty-four-hour wipe cycle, but one you can totally play to your advantage.

14: Running A Promo

Now that we've covered the two primary ways of deploying BookBub Ads—fast or slow, lest you forget my revolutionary taxonomy—let's get a little deeper into specifics. Here we are going to look at exactly *how* you use BookBub Ads to promote a freebie, a discount, or a launch. We'll also look at some logistical steps you can take to get the most out of your campaigns, and how best to target readers outside of Amazon, and internationally.

Pushing A Discount

A 99¢ deal is the natural candidate for a BookBub Ads campaign. It's the cheapest thing you can offer BookBub readers without being free, and is a very enticing price point with this audience—increasingly so, in fact, as the Featured Deals tend to focus more on $1.99 discounts these days. Obviously, this price is firmly in impulse-buy territory—and this price tag, along with a great cover that communicates the niche, can make it an insta-purchase for many fans of the genre.

All your ad graphic really needs to do is highlight that cover and the price-tag. Layering on additional aspects to your ad graphic can actually draw attention away from those two key elements, which you want to avoid. Perhaps include a tagline if you have a great one, but I recommend also testing an iteration without. And don't be afraid to make that price tag super prominent; subtlety wins no prizes here.

I prefer to see a CTR north of 2% for a 99¢ deal, as this generally delivers clicks in the sub-50¢ range, which I can work with. In case that raises any eyebrows from those of you doing quick calculations, profit will come from sell-through (to later books in the series), page reads (if the book is enrolled in Kindle Unlimited), and visibility (promotions can result in increased ranks and sales that will sustain for weeks, sometimes months, afterwards).

Of course, I should note that this kind of calculation refers to a limited-time 99¢ discount—a different calculus comes to bear when it's a permanent price point, such as an always-cheap Book 1 in a series. There you must figure out your own tolerance level, but you'll have the advantage of rolling out the ads slower and bidding lower, and using that to drive down your costs just as much as great CTR.

For the Countdown crew and anyone else running a limited time deal though, keeping those costs down is all about CTR. Presumably you will want to scale your campaign (as much as budget allows), so you might want to be seeing a good deal higher CTR than 2% for those initial tests.

On the morning of the first day of your promotion, roll out a quick $10 or $15 test to a group containing your best comp authors. Lump them all together—all those who have tested well. During testing, you might split up and test each author on their own, where possible. During a campaign, you need to do the opposite, so you don't get too much overlap between your campaigns. Each user will see each ad a maximum of four times, but that limit is set at the campaign level. The clock resets if you start a new campaign.

Set up the test campaign with the best quality image you can muster and limit the budget to $10 or $15. Select the option to serve as quickly as possible. Bid very aggressively on this test ad (i.e. higher than the highest end of the range recommended by BookBub). You want results fast because you will either be turning up the juice or re-jigging your image.

Remember that there will be a big serving spike in the morning—usually around 9:00am-10:00am EST (or 1pm to 2pm GMT) when the Featured Deals email goes out to Americans. Ideally, you want to have your quick campaign tests completed before then, so you can ride that wave if your ad is in great shape.

If the test results are good, turn up the juice by adding as much budget as you like to that test ad—no need to start a new campaign. If the results are sub-par, then you need to re-jig the image (your targeting should already be road-tested, so you don't need to mess with that). As always, restrict your testing to Amazon US even if your campaign is going wide and international, as that's the best proving ground. An ad there will usually do even better everywhere else, and once you are ready to scale up on Amazon US, you can safely add all the other retailers and markets you're targeting with this campaign.

I recommend only topping up the campaign budget with what you want it to spend that day. I find micro-managing this aspect and telling the system to serve as quickly as possible, works better than simply assigning an overall budget and date range, and asking the system to apportion it accordingly. But you can play with that if you prefer something more hands-off, for whatever reason— although I do find it's important to pay close attention to your BookBub Ads' performance, particularly at higher budgets when trying to scale aggressively. The more you scale a campaign, the more any flaws in the image (or targeting) will be magnified.

Promoting A Freebie

BookBub readers are quite price sensitive, which means they will respond wonderfully to free books. However, even well optimized ads with great targeting and images might only be delivering clicks in the 20¢-40¢ range. (To avoid confusion, I'm still talking about CPM ads, but ones that deliver an effective CPC in that range.)

While it's possible to make that work, especially with a long series with decent sell-through, or perhaps the page reads that a good free run can generate if you are in Kindle Unlimited, you need to be a little more cautious than with a 99¢ book as the promotion is not bringing in as much *immediate* cash to help with ROI.

Make sure you can afford what you're spending. Be careful that your ROI calculations aren't *too* aggressive. Aside from the danger of stealing from tomorrow to pay for today's ads, there can be cheaper places to get freebie clicks, quite frankly. Even though I'm very comfortable with BookBub Ads, I will lean on other sources quite heavily first. That means organic approaches like mailing list blasts/newsletter swaps and social media mentions will take prominence. And then when I want to bolster things with paid approaches—and I usually do—I'll reach for sites like Ereader News Today and Robin Reads and Book Barbarian and Freebooksy before dedicating any budget to BookBub Ads. There's a great list of promo sites here—*bit.ly/PromoSites*—which is rather handily kept up to date.

In terms of the image, again you will want to highlight the price tag—which I often do with an obnoxiously large FREE label. It handily fits on a button too if you want to go that route. Something high contrast will draw attention, of course; there's a reason why so many price tags are red labels with white text, or some combination of black and yellow. It really draws the eye.

With a free promotion, I'll be looking to get a good deal more than 2% CTR or else I'll know I should probably have another stab at the image (again, we're assuming author targeting has already been nailed down in the testing phase). While you don't want to go overboard with testing either, I often find that if I push myself, I can make yet another iteration to the image, which will see considerably better results. Sometimes I hit a killer image first time, other times it takes a few attempts. If your results are below where you want them to be, try to summon up the energy to have another go at it. Those efforts will pay off if you can improve that CTR. And you really need to do that to make a free promotion work with BookBub Ads. Mediocre CTR simply won't do, as your click costs will be too high *and* you're burning through precious audience too fast.

As with 99¢ promos, dole out your budget each day and set it to spend as quickly as possible. We'll deal with permafrees elsewhere, as the strategy is very different—with those you will be seeking to drive down CPM costs as well as increasing CTR. With limited-time promotions, however, it's much more about CTR. You need to bid reasonably high with the CPM to achieve any kind of scale in the short window of time you have.

Supporting A Launch

You can promote New Releases directly with BookBub Ads, although you must set expectations appropriately if that book is priced $2.99 or higher, as most new books will be. CTRs and conversions start to fall off from $1.99 upwards, so factor that into any calculations. Generally, I prefer to support a launch by discounting earlier books in the series and pointing my ads at those deals instead—a tactic I'll get into later on—but there will be situations where you may want to promote that new release more directly, and we'll explore those right now.

You have a number of approaches in terms of the ad image. I've tested them all, but feel free to conduct your own experiments. Generally, I find highlighting the newness of the book to be the best approach, but I've also had good results from highlighting a launch discount—e.g. where the new release might have a regular price of $4.99 but is discounted by a dollar or two for the launch. You might not always want to do that for a release, of course, but if you are taking that approach anyway with a launch, you can lean into it with BookBub Ads. But also perhaps consider testing a variant of the ad with a big NEW label where your price might be. I find that surprisingly effective.

When you're running those tests, you'll have to relax a little bit regarding what you might consider an acceptable CTR. Keep an eye on the Effective CPC column as well. I'm okay with a new release ad dipping below 2% CTR because I'm making much more per sale—meaning I can tolerate higher click costs. Plus, giving a new release a decent shove out of the gate can be a fruitful approach for many different reasons, and you may be willing to go into the red a little here as part of an overall strategy with this launch.

If you aren't getting good results from normally reliable comp authors with a new release ad, try focusing on just your own followers instead. They should be a lot less price sensitive than readers who are unaware of your charms. However, I don't recommend rolling that campaign out too quickly. BookBub will be sending a free New Release Alert to your followers. While I sometimes like following that up with an ad campaign targeting those same eyeballs again, and scooping up any stragglers, I definitely want to do that *after* the free email goes out.

In fact, I generally like running these ads towards the end of a launch window. You may be highlighting a free or 99¢ deal of an earlier book in the same series as part of your launch promos. A few days later, you can then hit that same audience again with an ad for the New Release. Play around with that approach; as you'll see later on, returning to the same well can be very fruitful … if you do it right.

Outside of Amazon

As I have stressed a number of times elsewhere, the markets outside of Amazon (and the US generally) are much more deal-starved and far less saturated. This makes very fertile ground for your deals and ads. You can get some remarkable CTRs on the non-Amazon retailers, which will in turn deliver exceptionally low CPCs. While these markets won't scale to the same level as Amazon—or anything close to it, quite frankly—collectively these markets can add up quite well.

In terms of actually managing a multi-retailer campaign, I tend to prefer setting up separate campaigns for each retailer I'm targeting, so I can have more direct input on how much of the budget gets spent in each location. You may want to dedicate less time to this and allow the system to determine that. It does a reasonable job in spreading the budget on a pro rata basis; it's just that sometimes I might want to be more aggressive in markets where I'm actively building up, for example. If you leave it in the hands of the system, it's simple to switch off one particular retailer anyway, in case performance collapses at Google but holds up at Barnes & Noble, for example.

Splitting things up might not be an option anyway. For smaller markets, you may not be able to run separate ads with your set of authors, as they don't have sufficient followers at those retailers to allow the ad to serve at all. If that's the case, the system will warn you during ad setup. To solve that problem, you'll have to either throw multiple retailers into the same campaign or beef up your author set. If you have a gold and silver set of authors, for instance, you can combine them for when you are running an ad outside of Amazon.

International Readers

A price tag in your ad image—which you will have in most cases, if you take my advice—can cause a few wrinkles here. America, Australia, and Canada all use the same dollars and cents symbols, so you can use the same ad graphic for campaigns in all these places—assuming your price or deal is the same everywhere. The pesky Brits though, with their pounds and pence, might need a quick redo. It's a trivial change in Canva, or easy for your designer to spin up, if you're outsourcing... as long as you remember to ask. Just remember to separate out those UK campaigns—you will need a fresh campaign if you are running a different graphic.

I find the easiest way to manage it, in practical

terms, is as follows: my main campaign targets Amazon USA only. I set up a separate campaign targeting Amazon UK, with that different ad graphic. And then I set up a third campaign targeting Canada and Australia, as I can use the same graphic in both markets and can make sure the ad gets served enough there. If I lump Canada and Australia in the same campaign as the USA, the American market will tend to gobble up nearly all of the budget quite quickly— especially if your ad goes up just before the Featured Deals email goes out to US subscribers.

It gets a little more complicated if you're running a campaign targeting internationally and outside of Amazon as well. You may have your own preferences here, but I tend to keep with the approach of running three campaigns—one to the USA, one to the UK with that different ad graphic, and one to Canada and Australia together, using the same ad graphic as America—and just throw in the non-Amazon retailers with Amazon in each territory. You may have your own preferences there, depending on how actively you are building up in different places, or how strong your existing readership is at various retailers.

Generally speaking though, you will see better CTRs and lower CPCs everywhere outside of Amazon USA… until the ad dies. And when it does, things can move pretty fast indeed. Either CTR will collapse or it will just stop serving—usually at the smallest markets first. BookBub is simply running out of people to show that ad to. Which means that if you want to keep pushing at Kobo Canada, or Apple Australia, for example, you might have to set up a fresh campaign and cast a wider net.

Just as having a permafree or permacheap Book 1 can be a crude but effective way of building up in new markets, slowly throwing different author targets at that always-discounted series entry point can be an effective way of unearthing new comp authors for future campaigns.

15: Tackling Problems

Of course, if you listened to me all the way through, this chapter would be nice and short, and I could take the rest of the day off. So... thanks.

While I can't anticipate every problem you'll encounter while running your first campaigns, after getting lots of feedback from my mailing list on the endlessly creative ways they were finding trouble, I have a pretty good handle on what the most common issues might be. I think it's a good idea at this point, before we move on to more advanced areas—those keenly anticipated ninja tricks and killer moves—to knock any problems on the head. Consider it a handy way to recap everything you've learned so far before you move on to those more complex techniques.

Generalized befuddlement aside—for which the only cure is to backtrack and take it a bit slower—the most common issues are:

(a) **Bland images.** Unfortunately, the gap between what we first think is good enough and what is actually good enough can be considerable. This is one of those things you will only realize in hindsight—like the fact that you were, indeed, too full for second helpings, or that the hilarious individual you encountered at 1:00 am in a dive bar was wrong for you all along. Oh well.

It's not that the images you are failing with are bad, as such. I'm sure many are within touching distance of being good enough. But these margins are tight.

Happy flipside: this means a minor tweak can greatly improve performance! Have another stab at that ad. When you think your image is good enough, try to make a couple of better ones; I bet you'll be able to do it. Pay particular attention to backgrounds and any accompanying text—these are the hardest to get right.

Text in particular—how do I say this diplomatically?—most people are just terrible at it. You can't just slap down any font and hope for the best. It needs to fit with the rest of the composition. This isn't easy, and is often what I spend most time on when making an ad. But once you crack this, you are on the way to developing your own *branding*, which is something you will be able to use in all sorts of areas. It's worth taking some care and getting this right. Try different fonts, alternative placements, messing around with the size. Look at great ads that use text well, and then try to reverse-engineer them. As with a book cover, the treatment of text is often what elevates a middling image and makes it truly great.

You also don't want those backgrounds too bland—a drab, monotone color is often what beginners first reach for (a mistake I totally made). But you don't want backgrounds *too* busy either, so the main attractions—i.e. the cover and offer—are lost in the noise.

And while we're talking about the cover, a 3D version usually gets better results. If you search for "3D cover generator" on Google you will get a bunch of free tools that do a fine job, where you can just upload your ebook cover and it will spit out a 3D version—often with a variety of options too. Ever wonder how authors made those fancy looking graphics with their book covers in phones and tablets? This is how.

See the BookBub Resources page on my web-site—*bit.ly/BookBub4*—for examples of successful ads and recommended tools.

(b) Overly broad targeting. This is comfortably the second-most common issue authors tend to struggle with, particularly for those of you with popular trad authors as comp authors. I'll tell you straight up: authors with a large number of followers are nearly impossible to target with BookBub Ads. You will invariably get better results by targeting mid-sized indies than giant trads. And if you need more authors, it's usually better to scoop up some smaller self-publishers and throw them together than attempting to target one of the bigger guns. And, yes, this still holds true if Beatrice Bestseller is your go-to comp author on Facebook and Amazon Ads, and is all over your Also Boughts, and is your bestest friend in real life (or locked up in your basement). Doesn't matter.

Unless you are incredibly lucky and win the targeting lottery (with odds to match, I suspect), the overwhelming likelihood is that the CTRs won't be good enough on a giant author like that. The audience is just too broad for it to work. Until BookBub develops better tools to slice-and-dice those bigger audiences, they will be too unresponsive in most cases, unless you are willing to tolerate low CTRs and exorbitant CPCs.

And if you just targeted by genre… ouch on that CTR. Go stand in the Circle of Shame until you promise never to do it again. You have some (re)reading to do.

(c) No offer. Honestly, we could all drive down to Tijuana and drink tequila until sunrise and get tattoos saying, "Always include an offer," and some of you would still run ads without an offer. Hey, I question myself most days, so I can't get mad when you do it too.

Lots of you will try to use BookBub Ads to sell full-priced books no matter what I say, so let's talk about that momentarily. This is a tough row to hoe—and I know my hoes! Remember where you are: this is a deal-hungry crowd, and your ad is popping up after a long list of free/99¢/$1.99 books, often from some of the biggest authors on the planet. Trying to flog them a $4.99 book at that point, from an author probably unknown to them, is tough. Every ad really needs some kind of offer to be successful. The most popular offers for BookBub readers are Free, 99¢, and then maybe New—pushing older backlist at full price is a real challenge.

It can be done, and *you* might be tempted into trying it when you hear people claiming they run profitable ad campaigns for full-price books on BookBub all the time. I think that statement needs a little unpacking though. Usually, they aren't making a *direct* profit from that ad campaign. More likely they are losing money in immediate terms, but they are estimating that each purchaser will go on to spend a certain amount of money on the rest of the series. These statements can be wildly inaccurate or overly optimistic, or they can be reasonably fair predictions based on solid data and past performance. Just know what you're dealing with here, and don't expect stellar CTR from higher-priced books. (Or don't expect great conversion if you don't mention the price.)

Personally, I find Facebook and Amazon Ads better for advertising higher priced books, and I like to keep my precious BookBub audiences for the promotions where they have most effect: those with discounts.

(d) CPC instead of CPM. Some of you will take one look at CPM Bidding and decide to use CPC instead. I know how it starts; you tell yourself you'll do your first campaigns with CPC Bidding as you understand that better, and perhaps switch to CPM Bidding when you have a firmer grasp of the system. I haven't injected you with thought-tracking nanobots; I just hear this a fair bit from BookBub neophytes.

And it's a big mistake.

Using CPC Bidding can create all sorts of problems, aside from bringing down my wrath. You will have issues getting your ad to serve, which means you can't get the data you need if you are testing. This can punch a giant hole in your plans if you're running a promotion. It usually ends up with the author getting more and more desperate and inching up those CPC bids to unsustainable levels, just to see if they can get the damn thing to serve. Then it does and suddenly you are paying more than a dollar a click. Now you have a new, money-shaped problem.

CPM Bidding is a little more confusing *at the start* but it's a much better way to learn the system. Plus, it delivers you cheaper clicks, stretches out your audience more, trains you to focus on improving CTR—and will probably do your taxes too, if you let it. Get over the initial confusion; it will pay off very quickly.

Besides, learning new things boosts your brain power and slows down cognitive aging, helping to stave off neurological issues later in life. So your gray matter will thank you, as well as your wallet!

(e) Budget too big. Some of you can be a little… impatient. This can manifest itself in a few ways. Like being too aggressive in the testing phase, dropping $100 like it's nothing, and then swearing off Book-Bub Ads when results are predictably tepid. Others will skip the testing phase altogether and jump right into running big campaigns targeting genre-buddies they are *sure* will be excellent comp authors on BookBub.

Yeah. That rarely goes well.

Don't skimp on testing. Not only will it save you pain in the long run, it also tends to unearth some surprising comp authors—targets that can add to your reach at other advertising venues too.

(f) Giving up on Amazon… or America. Wide authors are particularly susceptible to the former, international writers can be guilty of the latter. Both have the same root.

The US Kindle Store is the toughest place to target. Readers there are swamped with offers and have been for years. Books tend to be cheaper on Amazon than any other retailer in a general sense, and ebooks in particular are much cheaper in America than pretty much any other territory.

All this makes the US Kindle Store the most challenging market, with the most competition and the savviest level of competitors too. But that's because it is—by far—the most lucrative. Aside from being many factors bigger than the nearest comparable market, visibility is also worth lots more in the US Kindle Store. A sale there will have sale-babies, and lots of them if you do it right.

But you all know this. You don't give up on that market because you are unaware of the dollars to be had. It's because you are getting outgunned and squeezed out and are getting much better results in other markets with way less hassle too. I get it. But here's the thing: if you really want to scale, you need Amazon in play.

CTRs will always be better in the relatively deal-starved markets of Kobo, Apple, Barnes & Noble, and Google. Countries like Australia and Canada tend to have much higher priced books too. Combine both of those factors, along with the relative amount of saturation, and an ad to Kobo Canada or Apple Australia can get remarkable CTRs, at least initially. But they are much smaller markets and will only scale a little bit—meaning your ads can stop serving relatively quickly as the audiences can be quite limited.

To build big campaigns capable of shifting hundreds (or even thousands) of copies of your Book 1 to support the launch of Book 2 or 3, you really need the bigger markets involved. This is why I always do my first testing on Amazon, and restrict the serving to America. Yes, CTRs are usually lower there, and eyeballs are more expensive (and discerning, as they are saturated with deals). But a winning ad there will perform wonderfully well everywhere else, so it's the perfect place to hone something.

All that said, if you are just running a small budget campaign, and you are wide, then seek out the cheapest pockets of clicks where needed.

Those are the main problems I see authors encountering. But perhaps it's not you! Maybe it's me. I'm not breaking up with you, but if you are still struggling at this point, it might be that the way I'm framing things might not be quite clicking for you.

It's possible that coming at things from a different angle will help them fall into place, and I'm more than happy for this to be a group effort, so here are some alternative perspectives. Most of these are from the BookBub Partners blog—which has a wealth of information on all kinds of marketing topics, not just BookBub Ads:

1. Some straightforward and clear advice from Diana Urban at BookBub on how to run a split-test. *bit.ly/BookBub5*

2. A guest post from my own website written by Carlyn Robertson of BookBub on Clever Ways Authors Are Using BookBub Ads. *bit.ly/BookBub6*

3. This is a wonderful case study from bestselling author, and all-round smarty-pants, Cheryl Bradshaw on how she used BookBub Ads as part of an overall strategy to power herself to yet another USA Today Bestseller sash. I mean, come on. How many does she need? *bit.ly/BookBub7*

4. Need some more troubleshooting tips? *bit.ly/BookBub8*

5. Want a free calculator for figuring out ROI? BookBub has your back. *bit.ly/BookBub9*

6. Finally, as I know that misery loves company, here are the biggest mistakes authors are making with BookBub Ads. *bit.ly/BookBub10*

That should have you covered. Now it's time to enter the dojo.

PART VI

NINJA TRICKS...

After all those painful days chopping through wooden blocks *with your goddamn bare hands*, you've earned this moment. It's time to level up with some ninja tricks. Aside from selling lots and lots of books—and BookBub Ads are really good at that—there are some killer moves that can turn raining cash into a glorious money monsoon.

16: Also Bought Insurance

"A terrible beauty is born." William Butler Yeats was one of the first people to talk about Amazon's algorithms, and how their razor-claws of love can sometimes carelessly juggle a newborn book, even before the poor mite has developed that hard shell of bitterness essential to survival in world where—

Also Boughts. They are the public face of Amazon's book-blessing AI—part dream-maker, part widow-maker. But one you can... communicate with, in a sense. In case you don't know exactly what I'm referring to, I mean the strip of other books that appears under your book description on its Amazon page, headed with "Customers who bought this item also bought." Obviously that's quite unwieldy, so it commonly gets shortened.

I think of Amazon's system as a giant recommendation engine. One we can provide information to, and try to give it an accurate picture about our book, as well as the type of readers who should enjoy it. Or you can let the system guess.

(I don't like guesses.)

When I launch a book, I worry. Lil' newbie is out there all on its own, without the warming blanket of multiple five-star reviews (he says, in no way planting a seed). What if Amazon recommends this book to the wrong people? If they don't buy it, Amazon will stop bothering altogether, dooming me to a life of basement-living and noodle-slurping. Which is fine in your twenties, but just gets a little seamy at my age. Besides, the damp would play havoc with my extensive collection of feather boas.

I understand where Amazon is coming from, I should note. It has seven million ebooks at its cyber-fingers to push on any given day. And it likes to make money, as you may have heard. But this robot-powered ruthlessness can benefit you too—*if* you help it along a little. And BookBub Ads can do that, by ensuring the right Also Boughts attach to your book. Why is that so important? Let me explain…

If you really want to get your nerd on and dive into this stuff properly, you'll have to read my free book *Amazon Decoded*—but I'll include a summary here, so everyone doesn't go dashing off at once, leaving me alone here, talking to myself like some guy who never gets off the subway. Besides, pointing you elsewhere is extremely inconsiderate. Some of you might be reading this while on a camping trip with no wifi—although I'm not sure why anyone would do that when there are bears and spiders and serial killers and things that crawl into your ears and lay eggs. Hens? I live in the city, and might have some details wrong.

Anyway, Also Boughts are mysterious and infuriating and so very central to everything; they essentially power Amazon's recommendation engine. As already explained, Also Boughts are the strip of other books appearing on your product page on Amazon—not the advertisements (marked "Sponsored products related to this item") but the *other* strip. And rather than being a mere curiosity, or sometimes a nice way to discover books, this strip is representative of what Amazon's system thinks of your book—the particular kind of story it has it pegged as, if you like.

In short, if all the books in this strip are similar enough to your book, you're doing well and Amazon's system has a good idea of what type of book you have written; this helps inform them which customers might like it. But if all the books in this strip are very different from yours, you *may* have a problem, and Amazon's system could be recommending your book to all the wrong people. Uh oh.

Authors can spend a lot of time worrying about Also Boughts, especially for new releases. This isn't irrational or baseless fretting either; it's difficult to recover from Also Bought pollution for all sorts of reasons, and it is especially damaging when a book is brand new and hasn't built up any kind of organic sales history.

We could go down the algorithmic rabbit hole of Also Boughts forever—I barely made it back alive, you guys—but all you really need to know right now is this: it's extremely important to push your book to the right audience. This is especially important in the first couple of weeks of a new release when there is no real sales history. Otherwise, Amazon's system may get confused about what type of book it is (because it decides based on who the buyers are and what other things they have bought previously). If you start pushing your book to people who don't normally read in your niche—for example, if friends and family buy your novel, aiming to support you—this can actually hurt your book. As such, any tool that helps us encourage the *right* Also Boughts to appear is very welcome indeed.

Honestly though, despite my preference for BookBub, Amazon Ads are a slightly better tool for this job—mostly because you can drill right down and target by book. It's obviously beyond the scope of this text to teach you how to use Amazon Ads, but you might get some use from this quick-and-dirty guide I sent to my mailing list a while back—*bit.ly/BookBub11.* That said, Amazon Ads are notoriously unreliable, so it's good to have a Plan B either way.

BookBub Ads are perfectly placed to fill that role with their strong focus on author targeting. They do a much better job on that front than Facebook Ads, the other obvious alternative here. Facebook allows you to target *some* individual authors (and a tiny percentage of specific books) but coverage is very spotty indeed. If you have a list of 10 or even 20 comp authors, it's entirely possible none of them will be targetable on Facebook, even if they have thousands of Likes on their Page. BookBub, however, has most authors in its extensive database—anyone you might want to target, at least.

Before anyone objects, the absolute best way to ensure your Also Boughts are pristine is to ensure you are exclusively marketing to your true target audience—something I wrote a whole other book about, *Strangers to Superfans*—as well as avoiding any overly ambitious attempts to convert what you might call adjacent audiences. The best way to encourage *specific*

Also Boughts is to cross-promote with the author in question, often through something like newsletter swaps. However, that's not always an option. And even if you do have the luxury of cross-promoting with some of your comp authors, it's good to have some insurance in your back pocket—which is where ads come in.

Amazon Ads have the considerable benefit here of being able to target by book, but BookBub Ads are not without their specific advantages. The incredible responsiveness of the platform is a real boon in a scenario like this one, as you will be flying blind with Amazon until that sluggish reporting kicks in. One disadvantage of BookBub Ads that must be stressed, though, is the price sensitivity of its deal-hungry audience. They don't really like full-price books half as much, so I strongly recommend stressing the newness of the book over the price, particularly if it is above $2.99. Or a killer hook, if you have one.

You should anticipate lower CTRs when you can't lead off with a big discount as the offer you are stressing in your ad, and expect lower conversion rates too. That goes with the territory for higher priced books, so factor that into your calculations. But you might be happy to lose a little money to ensure the right Also Boughts get attached, and this kind of campaign has the happy side-effect of helping along your new release too—something you may already be prepared to invest a little in.

Besides, we'll make the money back later with some saucy moves.

17: Get Out Of Jail Free

I'm particularly fond of this trick as it was my original, primary use for BookBub Ads, and is still something I lean on regularly in one form or another.

While BookBub Ads are now a key driver of sales in every major campaign these days, I used to consider them more of a nice bolt-on. BookBub Ads were effective, but the audience seemed limited. As a result, the platform didn't have the ability (for me, at that time) to scale up effectively to make a truly meaningful difference to launches or other major promotions. But BookBub Ads always had that wonderful responsiveness, as well as the replicability and consistency they also still have today. Once your ads are optimized, of course.

This is the key advantage BookBub Ads always had over Amazon and Facebook, which made it a very useful tool even back when I would struggle to spend $500 in the week of a major promo, without the wheels coming off. This wonderful responsiveness meant that—once my ads were optimized—I could turn BookBub Ads on and off like a spigot, knowing roughly how many sales would gush out too. It had a predictability and reliability no other platform came close to... which meant I never included it in my marketing plans.

Say what?

I had another role for BookBub in my launches and promos: the firefighter. BookBub was my Get Out Of Jail Free card. I kept it in my back pocket and only whipped it out when something went wrong with a launch. And as I'm sure you all know, that happens more often than not these days, especially if your marketing plans are in any way involved.

Most of the platforms we use seem to be either permanently in beta to one extent or another, or constantly split-testing new features (and introducing new bugs), or just experiencing the kind of glitches that can easily knock a well-tuned promo off target. These things all seem to be a perma-feature of the landscape these days, and there's no real point bitching about it. Well, that's a lie. I totally bitch about it all the time; it's very cathartic! But there's no point expecting grousing to change the situation. I prefer *solutions* for that, and BookBub can be a bunker buster-shaped solution.

All sorts of things can go wrong when there are so

many moving parts. Maybe your email send didn't fire, or you're locked out of your account until Support gets back to you tomorrow. Perhaps a promo site you booked dropped the ball. Or maybe today is one of those times when your Facebook Ads get caught in review for a day or more, and customer service won't begin looking into it until twenty-four hours have passed. Or one of those times when Amazon decides to mess up your Countdown Deal and it's now starting a day late. Or a fellow writer who was supposed to send out a newsletter swap has a family emergency. Or *you* do.

These things can be minor issues in the normal day-to-day, but during a launch they can totally throw you for a loop, especially if you are trying very hard to string together five successive days of strong sales to tickle the ever-capricious Amazon algorithms into action. This is where Captain BookBub really can save the day, and get the girl too.

If you have your art assets to hand—always smart—and you have already figured out your targeting (which you will have done via the testing process outlined earlier), then you can knock up a BookBub campaign in a few minutes. And it will start serving very quickly after that, bringing you sales almost right away. (Remember that *reports* of those sales might take four or five hours to hit your KDP dashboard, and the respective clicks will take a little time to hit your BookBub dashboard too, but the ads will start serving very quickly indeed, generating immediate sales if they are optimized.) There is nothing else out there that can do that—and with the frequency that things *do* go wrong these days, it's very comforting to know you have that Get Out of Jail Free card in your back pocket. I find it takes a lot of the worry out of a launch, which can be stressful enough as it is.

Amazon Ads are simply unsuitable for the role unless you like taking giant big leaps into the darkness. Reporting is so lethargic there as to be insulting, quite frankly, given the money it generates. The whole platform is like a 1990s bad dream; I'm expecting Chandler Bing to walk in at any moment. Even if you throw up some quick ads on Amazon to stop a launch going off the rails, you have no idea if the ads are serving and working, or burning through money, before it's too late. But let's say you are extremely lucky and subsequently find out the ads weren't half-bad, you would still need a time machine to go back and scale them up to properly support your launch.

Reporting is much better at Facebook, admittedly.

Not *quite* as lightning quick as BookBub, but infinitely nippier than those slouches in Seattle, and more than adequate for these purposes. Facebook's indolence manifests itself elsewhere: either in the unpredictable review process (anything from hours to days, with patchy weekend coverage), the initial serving of an ad (sometimes it can take a few hours or longer for a campaign to get up to speed, unlike BookBub, which can seem to do so instantly), or its actual performance (Facebook's heavily touted machine-learning algorithms can take 24 hours or more—days, sometimes—before they really figure out how best to serve your ads).

I've been in the position quite a few times with Facebook where I've started a promotion on a Thursday and realized it needed something extra on Friday, but had a newly beefed-up campaign stuck in review all weekend long until someone finally got to it on Monday afternoon. By the time the ads hit full tilt on the Tuesday the campaign was pretty much over. Not ideal for when your balls are already in the fireplace.

You can be flexible with BookBub in a way that's trickier elsewhere. For example, let's say I have a $500 budget on BookBub Ads for a given launch. I might think that's a touch hefty for a Get Out Of Jail Free card, so I could allot $50 a day for the BookBub Ads part of my launch campaign for each of the five days I'm giving a strong push, and keep $250 of that in reserve. Then if something goes wrong on Day 1, 2, or 3, I'm ready—I can ramp up those BookBub campaigns in an instant and plug any holes in my launch. And if I don't hit any problems during my launch, I can just start ramping up the BookBub campaigns on Day 4 or 5 anyway, knowing that finishing strong on any promo is always welcome.

It's quite a bit harder to do that with Facebook and near impossible with Amazon.

When you're planning your next launch or big promotion, consider holding back at least some of that BookBub spend for your own Get Out Of Jail Free card. Even if you don't end up having to use it, you can drop that cash anyway towards the end of your promo period, and enjoy the benefits of a reduced-stress release.

I was going to say no-stress, but who are we kidding?

18: Filling The Funnel

There are innumerable ways you can market a book but, to return to my revolutionary nomenclature, they generally fall into two categories. The first is the kind of big, burst promotion the last chapter dealt with—examples would be the classic approach to launching a book where you try to condense sales around launch day/week, a KDP Select free promotion, a limited time discount, or a Kindle Countdown Deal. That's one way of marketing a book.

The other way is what I daubed drip marketing—where you have a constant steady stream of sales coming in—and a well-known example of that approach would be making the first book in a series either cheap or free.

Authors engaging in this kind of drip marketing often focus advertising on those cheap or free series entry points, usually engaging in some form of calculations with regard to what percentage of readers will continue on to subsequent books. This then allows them to advertise within certain parameters, with confidence that they will make their outlay back in the long run, as readers get hooked and complete the series.

If you have written a series—and, unless you are playing the author game on Ironman Mode, you really should—then you have a very clearly defined sales funnel. Book 1 is the top of your funnel, obviously, and there is a clear and logical progression to Book 2, and onwards to Book 3 and so on. Even if this is the type of series that can be read out of order, you will still be pushing that Book 1 all the time. Whichever is the latest book in the series will also be getting pushed, but will mostly be getting promoted to existing readers; Book 1 will be doing the hard work of finding you brand-new readers to feed into the top of that sales funnel.

In most cases, that Book 1 will be a reduced price—free or 99¢ or $2.99 are all popular price points for that first book—and the rest of the books in the series might be $3.99 or $4.99 or more, sometimes rising a little as they go along, sometimes not. Writers will play with price to see what works best for them overall in terms of some combination of bringing in new readers and maximizing income. Often the pricing will get more aggressive over time, and that Book 1 can get cheaper and cheaper until it is free, in many cases. Other authors will make that series opener free for an extended period, but when they feel like they have flogged that angle to death, they might put it back to 99¢ or even $2.99. That's the beauty of being the captain of your own ship— you can change course on a whim. That, and having two girls in every port, of course.

While some marketing push will be on that latest book in the series, authors will typically always have something pointed at that cheaper Book 1 to make sure there is a constant stream of fresh blood coming in at the start of the series—or the top of the funnel if you prefer. The lines aren't always 100% clear, but it's not that much of a leap to suggest that some of your tools are better at that job than others. To give a painfully obvious example, your mailing list—once you have a mailing list of any size—will always be the biggest driver of sales for any new release.

Conversely, those hardcore fans on your list have probably snaffled most of your backlist, and will be far less interested, in relative terms, in hearing that the first book in your series is free. If they are on your list, they've probably grabbed it already. (If you are having problems building a passionate list of readers, read *Newsletter Ninja* by Tammi Labrecque— *bit.ly/BookBub12*—you can see in the foreword to that book what adopting her principles did for my own career.)

On the other hand, a deal site like Ereader News Today, for example, is a much better place to find new-to-you readers who won't have heard of your cheap/free Book 1, rather than for pushing Book 6— particularly if it's not heavily discounted. And the same often goes for BookBub Ads, meaning that a great use for them is to have them slowly working away in the background, constantly bringing in new readers.

To make this work for you though, you need a slightly different mindset than when you are constructing the big blowout campaigns you might adopt for other purposes. Your approach to targeting and images should be more-or-less the same, but you'll have a little more focus than normal on bidding.

Remember when I said I don't really care about bidding, because with CPM Bidding, your focus should be on improving your ads and using increased CTR to reduce your CPC? That applies more to those burst campaigns. For drip campaigns, it's also important to have good CTR, but you will get best value from being less aggressive with your bids.

Again, this goes back to how ads are predominantly delivered. While BookBub sends all sorts of emails to users now, depending on their preferences, Featured Deals emails are still the main event—over 8 million emails a day for these alone. This kind of volume, understandably, drives most impressions of BookBub Ads. As such, the overall serving pattern of any BookBub Ads campaign is heavily skewed by the time of day BookBub sends out those Featured Deals emails, and the typical open patterns we see in such emails. You'll know this yourself from your own newsletter blasts, but as a *very* rough rule of thumb, you might see half of eventual opens come in that first hour, half that amount again in the next hour, and again in the next hour, and so on, like some radioactive half-life thing I'm too lazy to research.

This makes for a much more compressed serving schedule than Facebook or Amazon—which you will have noticed if you threw up an ad just before the email went out and watched your money vanish in an instant. What that means for drip marketers looking to fill the funnel of any given series is this: you can find great value when everyone else is out of budget. This is a popular tactic with Amazon Ads, but the window for finding such value is even greater here with BookBub because many advertisers can run out of budget a lot earlier in the day, meaning you can swoop in with a lower bid at that point and get much cheaper clicks as a result. If you only have $5 or $10 or $20 to spend on BookBub Ads in a given day, then this approach can make a real difference.

It might *sound* labor intensive, but it doesn't have to be. Earlier on I suggested a general approach to bids as follows: go high for testing to ensure you win the auction and get your results as quickly as you can; go medium for regular campaigns (where medium is the upper end of the range BookBub is suggesting for your genre); go low for drip campaigns, like we are discussing here.

I'll give you some concrete examples below, but I want to stress that they are just examples—not suggestions. The optimal bid for you will depend hugely on your genre, your author targets, the retailers and territories you choose, and then vary depending on not just the time of day but the time of year also (Valentine's gets pricey for Romance, Halloween for Horror and Urban Fantasy, Christmas for everything) and even the day of the week (publicists working for large publishers don't work weekends and prices drop!).

Let's give Mr. Theory a well-earned break and look at a hypothetical. Suppose you are an author of historical mysteries with fantastical elements, one with a time-travel angle like Diana Gabaldon's infinitely popular *Outlander* series. You might wish to target her followers, but as she has a staggering 344,091 of them, you are extremely unlikely to have any success doing that, as you will know from reading earlier sections of this book. Giant trad authors are near-impossible to target. You will probably get much more joy from targeting a successful indie author in the same space. Like Sarah Woodbury, for example, who has 11,383 followers—perfectly in the zone for you to target, assuming you do genuinely share an audience with her.

If you were running a big, blast campaign targeting followers of Sarah Woodbury, a bid below $10 would rarely be enough to get any kind of scale—at least not the level of serving you might wish for when doing something like supporting a Countdown Deal with a big budget promo. However, you might find that lower bids can work if you are running a smaller, always-on, drip campaign, slowly pushing the first book in your series. Let's say you have a budget of—to pick a random number—$15 a day. You might find that a bid of just $8 is enough to get served towards the end of the day when everyone else has spent their budget. This lower CPM will bring your click costs down, meaning you will be able to afford more clicks overall per day for the same amount of money.

At lower budgets you might even find that still lower bids will work—the smaller your daily budget, the further you can push this, meaning you can eke out some surprising value even on the most modest budgets. Just remember, the farther you go with this, the bigger the risk that your ads might not serve at all that day. However, you'll get a feel for the tipping point over time, and can adjust accordingly. Then, if you find this approach is working for you and bringing you in lots of new readers who go on to buy subsequent books, you can reinvest the proceeds in feeding even more people into the top of that funnel. And if you really are on very modest budgets, don't forget that tip about advertising on the weekend! Same goes for holidays. Corporate workers for large publishers can drive up the cost of BookBub Ads during the week when they are on the clock, which means prices can fall on Saturday and Sunday. Something to keep in mind if you are on a shoestring budget.

There are a variety of ways to calculate what kind of bids or budgets you can afford. As I said back in Chapter 6, some authors go more by gut, and others prefer to whip out the spreadsheets. Some of the latter will calculate everything they can, right down to expected sell-through percentages for each subsequent book in the series, as well as making adjustments for Kindle Unlimited borrows. There are various suggested formulas floating around too. BookBub put together a handy bidding calculator recently, which you can download here—*bit.ly/BookBub9*.

For an even more detailed approach to calculating ROI and bid thresholds and sell-through and all that, you should check out this guest post author Nicholas Erik wrote on my blog called How To Advertise And Sell More Books—*bit.ly/BookBub13*.

But if you aren't one for spreadsheets or sell-through calculations, don't worry. A solid gut instinct, well-fed with data morsels now and then, will serve you just fine too. You might have a strong sense that going above 80¢ a click puts you in the red, even with sell-through, and that's often enough to know, really. It depends how you like to operate.

To avoid confusion, I don't recommend testing in this manner—even if you are on a tight budget. To get good, clean data, you need that serving to happen fast, which means you need to bid aggressively. But once your author targets are nailed down, you can pivot to this cost-effective funnel-feeding approach and eke out value to your heart's content, where low daily budgets and low bids and high CTRs will do wonderfully well for you. Just remember, you'll have to increase those bids and budgets if you want to scale up.

This strategy can be extremely effective at slowly (or not so slowly, if you have more money to spend) feeding readers into the start of a series. They will then go on to read the rest of the series as long as you've done your job with Book 1, and once your end-matter neatly leads them to that Book 2, of course. Lots of ifs and buts there, which makes me wonder: what if there was a way to sell them the entire series in one go?

That *would* be something, he says, in a labored attempt at foreshadowing.

PART VII

...AND KILLER MOVES

Ninja tricks are fun and all, but it's time for The Big Reveal. I'm going to show you the *non plus ultra* of book advertising, a glorious trifecta of killer moves that will boost your BookBub Ad expertise to the stratosphere. This trio of tricks, which all neatly dovetail with each other, are so powerful I simply didn't believe the results when I first used them—they are that good. Used in conjunction, these killer moves allowed my CTRs to soar, drove ROI through the roof, and more than quadrupled my reach too. Or in layman's terms, these techniques allowed me to quadruple my spend on BookBub, all while getting a seriously better return for my money.

19: Turbocharge Series Sales

If you've read my book *Strangers to Superfans*, you know the challenge we face even after getting readers to click through to Amazon. We spend all this time and money getting our heads around all the various ways to market a book, and we sometimes think our job is done once we finally coax someone to our book pages.

Not so fast.

The sad fact is that most readers won't complete the transaction. And by "most," I don't mean slightly more than half. I mean nearly all of them.

A *good* conversion rate from a BookBub Ad is around 20%. While you are no doubt aghast at such a number, let me tell you this is higher than Facebook Ads and significantly higher than Amazon Ads, in my experience. Probably higher than anything out there, other than a Featured Deal or an email to an engaged list of your own fans.

But back to BookBub Ads. If 20% are purchasing, what are those other 80% doing?

Well, some probably have purchased also, and we are unfairly maligning them; they just haven't been tracked for one reason or another. For example, a growing problem for data-nibblers like myself these days is that phones are increasingly considered to be a decision device—the place where a reader might encounter your ad and click on the link and *decide* to buy. But that given reader might not actually *complete* the transaction until they get to their computer. Some people just don't like buying on phones. (I admit to this, even though it probably ages me as much as eating applesauce, collecting stamps, or regularly "resting my eyes.")

My own case of cultural progeria aside, many readers aren't logged in to all their accounts permanently on their mobile device, so their login isn't automatic and/or their payment information isn't saved. Or sometimes they just find the buying experience on the mobile version of the site too annoying or confusing—remarkably common, even today. However, that doesn't come close to describing everyone.

The unpalatable truth is that most readers actively choose not to complete the transaction you desire so much, either by closing the tab or clicking away somewhere else. And Amazon provides plenty of ammo for the latter—as I mentioned in *Strangers to Superfans*, when I launched a book recently, between the sponsored results and Also Boughts and other advertisements Amazon had slathered everywhere, I counted 248 other books advertised on my page.

That's a *lot* of shiny distractions.

I'm sure you have noticed all these ad placements encroaching on "our" book pages, but one positive development in the other direction—for once!—was the roll out of Series Pages. Not only did this development claw back some key real estate for authors, it also acted as a handy visual cue to readers that this was, in fact, a series and, crucially, that there were other installments already out and available for purchase, not merely on the drawing board.

Clicking through to these Series Pages revealed something else too: a nice big, fat button at the top, where readers could buy the entire series in one go. The system was even intelligent enough to factor in where a reader had Books 1 and 2, but was yet to purchase Books 3 through 5, and show the correct price to purchase only the remainder. Pretty nifty. (Note: if you are outside America and viewing the US Kindle Store, you will not see this handy Buy button, but it's there, I promise!) And here's the best bit: there are no ads on these pages. No Also Boughts. No distractions.

I lied.

Here's the best bit.

You can run BookBub Ads to these pages. *Oh yes.*

It's a little-known fact that you don't have to run a BookBub Ad to a standard book page. You can point a BookBub Ad pretty much anywhere, as long as the purpose of the ad is to sell books. It's not a requirement to use the search box at the start of the ad creation process to associate a campaign with a specific book in their database. That's merely a courtesy to authors, one that auto-generates links to save them some time scrabbling around, and helps track book-specific performance in your stats. It's not actually necessary. In fact, it's not even a requirement to point your campaign at a retailer—you can run BookBub Ads to your website if you want, although it's not something I particularly recommend.

To create a Series Page ad, all you need to do is copy the link to your Series Page from Amazon and pop it in the box where you would normally put the link to your regular book page. Make sure to test it, as you normally would (he says in hope, wondering if Pavlov ever felt so forlorn).

Returning for a moment to what BookBub permits, there are *some* restrictions with BookBub Ads—mostly covering various kinds of nefarious activity.

The only thing that could trip up those running a clean business—the only people I care about, quite frankly—is the prohibition of lead-generation ads. While you can run ads to your website, if the main purpose of those ads is to drive sign-ups, that's not permitted, even if you are doling out a reader magnet. Grouse if you want; their house, their rules.

I can confirm that ads pointing to Series Pages are most definitely permitted though—and thank heavens for that, because running these ads (using both Facebook and BookBub) is by far the most effective marketing tactic I've deployed in the last couple of years. They are so much more powerful than just focusing on that first book, because a remarkable number of readers will actually use the Buy button at the top of the page to grab the whole series at once—particularly if you run deep discounts across the series.

Of course, I'm far too stupid to come up with something this clever. This incredibly smart trick was invented by Phoenix Sullivan—author, publisher, data hound, algorithmic savant—and shamelessly stolen by me. I'm so dumb that I didn't realize just how powerful this trick would be, at first. Part of that is not completely my fault; I'm based outside the US and can often see small differences with the US

Kindle Store for territorial reasons. For example, these rather handy Series Pages look a little different to me—they don't have that crucial button above the fold where readers can one-click the whole series. Which meant I didn't understand why Phoenix was raving about them quite so much.

But once I spun up my first proper campaign, I soon realized Series Page ads were a complete gamechanger. Remember, Series Pages have no Also Boughts and no Also Vieweds and no Amazon Ads taking up space and enticing readers away—apart from a couple of general product placements that are barely visible and not going to tempt many readers, unless they are desperately in need of a windcheater.

It's the polar opposite of our regular book pages these days, where the amount of showy distractions seems to increase every month. On Series Pages, the entire focus is on *your series*. And, not only is there a big obvious button encouraging readers to buy the whole series with one click, the system is even smart enough to recognize if you own some of the books already, and updates the price required to purchase the remaining installments accordingly.

As you might expect, the conversion rates on Series Page ads are simply phenomenal. The fewer distractions on these pared-back pages really closes the sale. I also think there is value in displaying the entire series at once to readers, particularly if you have at least a few installments released. Power readers have been burned repeatedly over the years by publishers dropping a series, or authors slowing down production for whatever reason. Readers like to know they can really get their teeth into something, and not endure interminable waits for subsequent volumes (this geek grumbles, still scarred from *Wheel of Time*).

The ability to purchase the whole series with one easy click means that Series Pages can be real money-printers once you start pointing ads their way. But something even more remarkable happens if you also run deep discounts across the entire series at the same time: an amazing amount of people will buy *all of the books at once*—to levels you simply won't believe until you try it.

I should note that the extent to which you will experience the latter effect is dependent on how aggressive you are with those price discounts. It operates very much like normal sell-through, just in a more immediate manner. With normal sell-through, you might have already noticed that it's heavily influenced by the step up in price between one volume and the next. For example, if you have a free first in a series and the sequel is priced at $4.99, that's quite a big step up and you will see a negative impact on sell-through—at least on *immediate* sell-through. The power of your writing will sell that $4.99 eventually, but readers will probably restrict themselves to downloading the freebie until they become fresh converts to your wondrousness. However, if you reduce that step up in price to $2.99, you will see immediate sell-through improve. Then, perhaps if you are running a promotion and have that second book at 99¢ temporarily, you will invariably see another uptick again in immediate sell-through.

So it goes with Series Page ads, except it happens *all at once*.

Tweaking the above example slightly, let's say you have a four-book series. The first book is free, and the rest are $4.99 each. If you run Series Page ads with that price structure, you will see a lot of people grabbing the freebie—it only costs them a click, after all—but you won't see quite so many grabbing the whole series or making any purchases beyond that first book. Not right away. They may do so, further down the road, whenever they get around to reading the free book, *if* they get around to reading the free book. A perennial problem with freebies is that readers have no real skin in the game, and it's easy just to add these free downloads to the ever-growing TBR (reader shorthand for a To Be Read pile) and forget they exist. But there are ways to circumvent that.

Let's say you run a Kindle Countdown Deal on that Book 2, making it 99¢ temporarily, and then run ads to the Series Page. What happens then? You'll get more people buying the whole series, and lots of those who are reeled in by the freebie also picking up Book 2 as well because it's firmly in impulse buy territory. But you won't get so many also buying Book 3 right at that moment because they hit the wall of that bigger step up in price to $4.99.

Two things can counter this. First, you can graduate those steps up in price. Again, modifying the above example, you could have Book 1 free, Book 2 at 99¢, Book 3 at $1.99, Book 4 at $2.99.

These are all temporary prices, I stress; I'm not suggesting this as a permanent approach at all. I don't want any confusion on that front. But this kind of temporary price structure can work extremely well for Countdown Deals or other time-limited discount promotions, such as supporting a launch, because once you reduce the steps between the prices you greatly increase immediate sell-through.

Obviously, the case for such deep discounts is stronger for those enrolled in Kindle Unlimited, but wide authors can experiment with this approach also—particularly those who have a backlist that's gone stale and little to lose. You might be surprised what can happen, even with the fustiest and mustiest.

And you can go further too. I was managing a promotion for another author who wanted to get sales going on a backlist series that had been flogged pretty hard via conventional means, selling an incredibly number of copies over a several year period. We were both curious whether the market was tapped out for that series (it had previously sold very well indeed before tapering off recently), or whether he had just exhausted standard approaches, as rank had slipped a bit, and regular promotions weren't doing much to change the picture.

I decided to try something really aggressive, not knowing how it would pan out: all nine books in the series for 99¢. I tried to get some of the discount sites on board to try something a little different and link to the Series Pages, but they weren't too keen on the idea—possibly because it was new or weird or messy, or maybe because the lack of Also Boughts might affect their affiliate income, I don't know. Either way, they weren't interested. Which meant everything would rest on the Facebook and BookBub Ads I would be running directly to the Series Pages.

I really wasn't sure how it would go but the results

were astonishing. Not only did all nine books in the series jump into the Top 1000, they did so *in lockstep*. The series had been stretched out between 20,000 and 50,000 in the rankings, but they now were bunched tighter than the starting-line of the Mega-City One Marathon—i.e. all within 50 ranks of each other; it was *eerie*.

Comments started appearing under the Facebook Ads, readers saying they had grabbed the entire series in one go, or they had bought the last five books they had yet to purchase—which was the most incredible social proof you could ask for, all now appearing under the ads to prospective readers. The BookBub Ads performed amazingly well too, with very high CTRs and brilliant conversion rates, contributing thousands of sales over the week of the promo.

Here's the crazy part: we had tried pushing this series to the *exact same audience* a couple of months beforehand, in the form of three box sets of three books each—very competitively priced at 99¢, $1,99 and $2.99 respectively—and the response was lukewarm (let me remind you this was a big series from a bestselling author). But when those same readers were presented with a Series Page ad selling all nine books for 99¢ each they swarmed all over it *even though it was costing them nearly three dollars more.*

Maybe getting nine distinct things just felt like a better deal; I don't know. What I do know is that it works.

I have since used this trick multiple times to great effect (thanks Phoenix!), and it's one of the most reliable tools at my disposal; deploying it has led to stunning results with Kindle Unlimited and a whole string of All-Star bonuses for authors I have worked with. But there are a couple of challenges you will face.

The first is in terms of designing the ad. It's difficult enough to come up with an enticing ad that communicates both the genre and the offer in a striking manner, all inside a 300x250 pixel box, without having to do that for nine bloody books at the same time, let me tell you. After testing numerous approaches, I find that shoehorning all those covers into the space is the most effective in terms of CTR (conversion too), probably for all the reasons why that tends to work well with a standard ad.

I'll be blunt: this is not easy. Your first designs will probably be terrible, and you might not even know how terrible until you show them to someone who will give you a truly honest opinion (I recommend having at least one Australian or Eastern European friend). This is definitely one case where you might want to outsource to a pro. Even when I had gotten to the point where I could design promo graphics comfortably in Canva, I still hired these jobs out. These days, I do them myself, but they are still very fiddly—even with lots of successful attempts under my belt.

The second challenge is even more difficult to deal with and it pertains to the Series Pages themselves. When you release a new book in a series, Amazon automatically updates the Series Page to include the new release. Problem is, the process of adding a new book to the Series Page can take that Series Page offline for a while, and all anyone clicking on your ads will see is Amazon's 404 Pages. That period can be anything from a couple of hours to a few days—and obviously it's not good if you are spending money on ads that only serve to introduce people to the charming dogs who now seem to run Amazon.

To assuage your concerns slightly, normally the Series Page goes down for just a few hours and then returns with the new release *in situ*. But this is Amazon, where glitches and delays of all kinds seem to be getting more common, so it's good to have a Plan B, and take precautions too.

In terms of the former, have some replacement

ads ready to go on BookBub (and Facebook, if you are advertising there). Have your graphics ready, in other words, and the campaign itself can be put up in a few moments once you have your images to hand.

Regarding the latter, you must try to encourage the Series Page to update as soon as possible. This means making sure your series metadata is pristine (i.e. that you name your series the exact same way in the metadata field for each installment). It might also mean harassing KDP's customer support to update the Series Page as soon as your newbie goes live. And I'd also recommend building a few days' lead-time into the release plan—by that, I mean aiming for the book to go live a few days before you start promoting it to anyone.

I know some authors routinely build that kind of slack into their launches anyway; I'm just noting it for those who sail closer to the wind. An extra few days can make all the difference, meaning the Series Page either updates before you start your launch proper, or it happens on Day 1 or 2. Definitely better than the Series Page going down on Day 4 or 5, pulling your most effective player from the game during the final quarter. I hope that American football metaphor worked because I spent like ten minutes on the internet figuring it out, and completely lost my train of thought.

Anyway, before the Series Page updates, you can still run ads pointing at it, but you have to watch them keenly and keep checking the Series Page. Remember that you're running a risk by doing this, and could be spending money sending people to a page that's down. It's a gamble, but once the Series Page updates you should be set. (I'd still recommend waiting an hour or so to ensure it's stable, as it can glitch out a little directly after.)

Series Page ads are worth the hassle though—yes, they are powerful enough that I would actually push a launch back a few days and try to trigger that Series Page update early, even if it did cost me a few days of that Hot New Release status I love so dearly. They really are that effective. But if your tolerance for risk is so low that the thought of the Series Page going down gives you the heebie jeebies, then just use Series Page ads for backlist promotions; the only time these pages go down is when you launch a new book in the series, so if the series is actually complete, you never have to worry about that again. Kind of like a vasectomy, but for your problems.

I hope you get a lot of joy from Series Page ads. I've found they can really move an entire series at once, which is quite a remarkable thing to witness.

I'm excited at the thought of you guys doing it too! It's so great to have a tool that can effectively move those troublesome middle children of a series, and give you one single place to focus reader attention when promoting the series as a whole. Sometimes you're speaking to a mixed audience of existing readers and prospective ones. Having a Series Page link to drop, instead of wrestling with pushing the opening book, or the newest, is very useful indeed. And being able to sell several things at once to the same clicker does absolute wonders for ROI.

Turbocharge the sales of an entire series at once by sending readers to a page where they can't get distracted by hundreds of ads pushing other authors' books? Sign. Me. Up.

Now, how do we top that?

20: Riding The Launch Slipstream

A common and effective promotional tactic is to discount backlist to help move frontlist. For example, if you're launching Book 3 in a series, running free or cheap deals on the earlier installments will obviously help push the new release. But what you can *also* do is use frontlist to push backlist and use that sexy new release to flog earlier books in the series.

I love synergy, and I adore spillover. Read-through is great, and immediate sell-through is even better again. Why? Because readers—right away—have more skin in the game. If someone downloads a free or 99¢ series opener, they may read it that day... or it may sit on their Kindle forever—in a literal sense, as in they may *never ever* get to it. Readers often report that they have dozens of unread books on their Kindle, mostly free or cheap books they grabbed during a sale. That number can grow to hundreds of unread books for power readers or bargain hunters. Realistically, they will never open most of them. Data from retailers like Kobo backs up these anecdotal reports, especially with regard to free books.

Does that mean you should avoid those tactics? Absolutely not. They are simply too effective to ignore. But if there is anything you can do to prevent *your* book languishing in an ever-growing TBR pile, then you should grab it with both hands.

Now, I don't have any data on this exact technique; I don't even have dressed-up anecdotes to support my claims. This is firmly in the area of *theory*—I want to be clear on that. But my strong sense is, after deploying this myself for a couple of years now, is that if you can flog multiple installments to the same reader at once, there is a much greater chance they will jump on that series right away, rather than letting it gather virtual dust on their device.

Which is what you want, obviously.

Assuming you are with me so far—stop making that face, Becky—let's look at some ways of triggering immediate sell-through of this kind, where we sell several installments of a series at once to readers to encourage them to *truly* commit to reading it.

Well, we've already covered one stellar way of doing this in the last chapter. Series Page ads are a wonderful way of using backlist to push frontlist, and turbocharging sell-through by making it happen all at once. Obviously, you can further support those efforts with Facebook Ads—that's beyond the remit of this book, but if you sign up to my mailing list at *DavidGaughran.com* you'll get tons of free advice on those.

You can also bolster these efforts by pushing the Series Page deals to your mailing list—reducing the number of links in your email always helps you avoid Spam filters and the Promotions tab—and also by posting the Series Page links to your Page and/or blog as well as anywhere else you regularly promote.

Doing this doesn't just lead to great CTRs and lower CPCs and better conversion and increased sales and *immediate* sell-through, it also tickles the Amazon algorithms like nobody's business. Every one of those mass-sales of multiple installments strengthens the connections between those series books in Amazon's recommendation engine *and* encourages its system to email readers who have already started it, usher them through the series, and recommend it to new readers for good measure too.

All of this is highly desirable for all sorts of reasons, and the benefits just keep multiplying the longer the series is.

There are a couple of tools that are pretty effective for pushing new releases right now, but that we have little influence over. Both Amazon and BookBub send

New Release Alerts to your followers. Amazon's approach is typically opaque. It doesn't tell you when it's going to send out the email. You can't even estimate it either, as sometimes it goes out during launch week, but other times they don't bother sending it until Week 2 or 3. I've even seen them send out so-called new release announcements over six weeks after the launch of the book, which is stretching the definition a little.

Sometimes Amazon doesn't send out the New Release email at all, and will claim it did, even though you have proof to the contrary (he says bitterly, listening to country music). Authors have no control over this at all. In fact, Amazon is so secretive that it won't even disclose how many readers follow you. This reflexive secrecy is ridiculous—this is hardly proprietary information—and acts as a massive disincentive to authors encouraging readers to follow them on Amazon.

BookBub's approach is much friendlier, although authors don't have total control here. We can see how many readers follow us (indeed, anyone can—it's publicly viewable). We can also submit our latest books to them to ensure a New Release Alert actually gets sent out (which they invariably do, aside from some restrictions around things like box sets). And we can see the date that it's going out in our interface (usually a handful of days after a book is launched/submitted). Which is all great! It means we can plan.

Those emails are going to your BookBub followers, who should be your core readers, unless you have used competitions or other inorganic means to aggressively build those up. This generally means that, assuming you have a non-trivial number of followers, that email send announcing your launch will have a measurable effect, something you can and should plan around, especially if you launch books in the manner I recommend: seeking to have a consistent or moderately increasing number of sales each day, over a multi-day period. You don't want any unaccounted-for spikes throwing off your careful planning.

You also don't want to miss out on a golden opportunity, because these New Release Alerts are *wonderful* places to advertise.

Think about the usual Featured Deal emails. Most readers are signed up to multiple genres, so their email will invariably contain several books at minimum, meaning your ad is quite far down the page—probably unseen by most. The New Release Alert has *one* book in it. Yours. And that ad slot is above the fold, no scrolling needed for it to be seen.

Which makes it the most perfect place for a Series Page ad.

This is how it works. Let's say you are launching the fifth book in a series. Normally, BookBub's New Release Alert will go out on maybe Day 2 or Day 3 of your launch. You will know in advance, to a certain extent, as BookBub will email you—usually just the day before. Currently, New Release Alerts only get sent to your American followers, but that should be the lion's share anyway. Plus, it's free. Hard to quibble.

On the day of your New Release Alert, make sure you're running an ad targeting yourself. (For many authors, this tends to be good practice anyway—not all of your followers will own all your books yet, and they can be a very responsive audience to any discount.) Make absolutely sure you bid high on the ad targeting yourself. You don't want anyone else stumbling into that prime spot, above the fold, visible to all your followers. Design the ad so that it's pushing the series as a whole (you can use the same graphic you're using for your series page ads to other author targets). Sit back and enjoy!

Wait, I hear some grumbling at the back. One moment...

My patented Objection Coagulator is spitting out

the following: "You're already pushing us to discount not just one book aggressively, but an entire series at once. I thought the point of discounting an early book in a series was to act as a kind of loss leader where you would make your money back on selling them the rest of the series at higher prices. And, not only that, but here you are pushing this to your core fans, who are surely going to purchase anyway—people who are more than happy to pay full price too."

I understand the objection completely. In fact, I've been an advocate for higher prices for all the time I've been self-publishing. Higher *list* prices. I'm also a fan of aggressive discounting for promotional purposes, which has all sorts of uses. In this particular case, you're trading probable future sales at full price, for even more likely discounted sales right now. What makes that worthwhile?

During a launch or backlist promo you are seeking to compress sales during that period, so as to achieve the highest rank possible over the longest potential period. You're seeking to maximize your visibility, not just during the promotion itself, but afterwards too (when those books *will* be full price, and still selling well, if you do it right).

And, of course, a corollary effect of all these sales

and ranks and chart positions and visibility is something else rather welcome and lucrative: a flood of recommendations from Amazon to customers in the form of either emails or on-site recommendations.

(I tend to focus on Amazon in these examples because no one else has a recommendation engine or ecostructure quite like Amazon, and visibility on Amazon is worth several factors more than visibility anywhere else for all sorts of reasons—read my free book *Amazon Decoded* if you really want to get into that topic.)

This equation hasn't changed in all the years since the ebook boom began; the only difference is that the rewards for achieving visibility have grown exponentially—which has made it quite the arms race these days as authors engage in increasingly sophisticated marketing strategies to try to squeeze out as much visibility as possible.

Yes, these deep discount arguments are all much more powerful for authors in Kindle Unlimited, and thus exclusive to Amazon, but visibility in the Kindle Store is valuable to any author. In other words, the very size of Amazon means that promotions should invariably be optimized for Amazon, regardless of whether you are exclusive or not.

This doesn't mean you should always discount

aggressively—I'm most certainly not suggesting that. But if you have a series that isn't moving through conventional means, one which has slipped down the rankings and can't be resuscitated, or one where you have exhausted all the usual means for promoting and the usual venues are tapped out, or one which is gathering dust because you don't know what to do with it, or one where you want to make very aggressive plays in support of a launch, then consider an approach like this.

It can be remarkably effective.

21: Do It Again (And Again)

Audiences can tap out pretty quickly, especially if you push them too hard. If we run the same book at the same price to the same audience, we are unlikely to get anything like the same results unless significant time has passed. If you regularly hit your entire mailing list two days in a row with the exact same offer, sure, you'll pick up a handful of people who either missed yesterday's email or didn't complete their purchase as they were distracted or whatever, but most of those people on our list will have acted the day before (or decided not to act—either because they aren't interested or because they already own the book).

It's pretty much guaranteed that you will annoy more people than you will catch with that second pass, and it's a very unsustainable way to run a mailing list. (That's not to say you can't do repeat sends under any circumstances; you can. Just be artful and/or make sure there is something else of genuine value in any subsequent email.)

Facebook Ads can be a little different. Facebook often recommends showing an ad four times or more to a given user, although I must say I disagree, at least for our business. Generally speaking, on Facebook we tend to also be advertising deals: free books, 99¢ books, series deals, box sets, or otherwise discounted books. Even when we are pushing a full-price book, like a $4.99 new release for example, that's still very cheap compared to many other products (or traditional publishers). It's a de facto discount, even at full price. And infinitely cheaper than many other types of product advertised on Facebook.

A customer is unlikely to need three or four opportunities to consider a purchase at that price point; they are either interested or not. As such, I tend to limit the frequency of ad viewings on Facebook to twice. If someone sees an ad for my 99¢ deal or freebie twice in their feed and isn't interested enough to click through, I don't think a third pass will convince them. This isn't a bloody sofa they are buying.

BookBub Ads is a little different. The system puts a hard cap on how much it will serve any ad to a customer of four times. I understand the campaign limit used to be three viewings, but BookBub nudged it up to four a while back. You might assume this was a self-serving move, but it really does work better this way.

Think back to how BookBub Ads are predominantly served to users—at the end of a long list of other deals, in an email. Once someone opens that email, your ad will be served, a pixel will fire, and that open on the reader side will be recorded as an impression on your dashboard—even if the reader doesn't scroll down far enough for the ad to be physically visible on their screen. You will see an impression on your dashboard which counts as a serving to that user, but there will be no click or sale—obviously, as they didn't even see the ad.

Because of this, BookBub is highly unusual in that serving these ads to customers four times doesn't really result in a decreased performance. And I'll go even further than that: because of how ads are served to readers, and because of how impressions are counted, I find that showing them the same ad *even more times* will fly.

In practical terms, this means that when a campaign has run its course and serving has slowed down or CTR has plummeted too far (whichever comes first), I can simply copy the whole campaign and start again… and get *very* similar results the second time around. The frequency cap of four viewings is tied to each individual campaign; if you copy and restart, you will also start the clock again on that, so the system will start showing your ad to all those people once more. On top of that, a re-run will also catch the many, many people who just didn't open their email on the previous day you were advertising—not everyone checks their email all the time, we might often forget. Some people even go outside!

To get best results for any kind of re-run, I think a slight tweaking of the image helps. I don't think wholescale revision is wise at this point, I just might switch up some of the colors. For example, if I've used white text on a red background for my button or price tag or offer, I might switch to a yellow/black combo the second time around, to try to catch the eye of those who might have skipped over it during round one. It seems to help. So much so that I can often eke out a third pass to the exact same audience by inverting that yellow/black.

I know, it's crazy!

I have a whole system down now where I make up three iterations of my (final, tested) ad graphic in advance, so I have everything lined up and ready to go when my initial campaign hits a wall and needs a reboot. This means I can spend more aggressively in the first couple of days of a launch, or Countdown

Deal, without worrying about how many arrows I have in my quiver, as I can replenish them easily.

There you have it. These trickster triplets are immensely powerful when used in tandem: Series Page ads to your target audience, hitting the New Release Alerts to your followers with Series Page ads underneath too, and then running the campaigns again (and again). This will allow you to double or triple your effective spend on BookBub Ads, and greatly improve your ROI too as you watch an entire series climb the rankings.

I trust you will find these strategies profitable.

About

David Gaughran is finally back living in Dublin after spells all over the world, including a house in Peru with no roof; he's still trying to get the sand out. He has written a bunch of other writer books you might like.

Let's Get Digital: How To Self-Publish, And Why You Should is highly recommended if you want to learn how to publish professionally and find your first readers, while also serving as a handy primer on the industry, covering topics like piracy, disruption, scammers, myths, and the ever-growing influence of Amazon.

Strangers to Superfans: A Marketing Guide to the Reader Journey is a revolutionary new approach to book marketing, teaching you how to map out the journey your Ideal Reader talks in their transformation from being someone who is unaware of your work, to being the kind of fan that does the selling for you by recommending it to anyone who will listen.

Amazon Decoded: A Marketing Guide to the Kindle

Store breaks down the ever-mysterious Amazon algorithms, teaching you how to optimize your metadata and marketing campaigns to trigger Amazon's system into recommending your book to its millions of customers. And it's available as a free download at *DavidGaughran.com*.

If you enjoyed *BookBub Ads Expert*, please consider leaving a review online. Even a word or two would be more helpful than you know.

David sends out weekly tips and tricks to thousands of authors every Friday, as you may have guessed from subtle asides placed sparingly throughout this text. If you want to continue the discussion on finding readers and building audience, make sure to sign up to his list (and grab your free book!) at *DavidGaughran.com*.

And if historical fiction is your thing, David is also the author of *Liberty Boy*, *Mercenary*, and *A Storm Hits Valparaiso*. You can read more about all of those—and get links to the various retailers where they are available—at a separate website *DavidGaughranBooks.com*. He's also writing science fiction under another name but hasn't unmasked himself *quite* yet.

Finally, please feel free to follow him on Twitter, get in touch on Facebook, or send him an email. He will answer you personally... which may be a pro or a con. You can find links to all those places, and a contact form, at either of the above websites.

Author Note

This is a very exciting moment for me as this moment marks the end of one phase in my career. I've been exclusively focused on author education for the last couple of years: updating my guide to self-publishing for those taking the plunge, breaking down the Amazon algorithms in a reader magnet to boost my mailing list, researching the forces that encourage (and prevent) readers becoming raving fans of your work, and now, finally, publishing this book on the fastest growing book marketing platform on the planet. And now I'm done. For a while at least. I'll be taking a break from writerly books and diving into fiction full-time for a good, long stretch. Although, maybe I'll sneak out another book for authors in-between novels *if you behave.*

I can make those snap decisions with the knowledge that I have a crack team I can pull together for any such project. Tammi Labrecque is the best possible editor in the world for a book like this because not only is she a skilled editor who doesn't jump out the window after replacing "that" with "which" four thousand times, she's also an author herself and knows these topics inside out. Any remaining errors were undoubtedly introduced by me after Tammi had finished her edits, and I broke my promise to stop fiddling. Alexios Saskalidis will probably need years of therapy to get over the amount of revisions I requested on this cover design, but he dealt with it the way he always does—with humor and professionalism, waiting patiently until I admitted he was right all along! Paul Salvette of BB eBooks handled the print layout and did a wonderful job, and I did stellar work with the ebook edition. Go me.

But this isn't just about me, as amazing as that ebook formatting was, he says, the room nodding in unison as they recall his immaculate chapter headings and perfectly formed Table of Contents. A whole army of writers made this book happen. And I don't mean that in a mushy Oscars speech kind of way; it's actually true!

This book started as an eight-part series I did for my mailing list. The original plan was to add a bit more info, throw in a couple of ninja tricks I had held back, and then publish a quick-and-dirty, guide to BookBub Ads. Then I made the mistake of emailing my list and asking them how *they* were using the platform, the kind of problems they had encountered, and what my emailed episodes hadn't covered in sufficient detail.

Around that time, I started drinking again.

I kid! I never stopped. But there were *so many emails*. Once I had waded through them, I realized that the book would have to be torn apart and started again. But that means you have in your hands a much more comprehensive guide to the platform. Essentially, it's a *de facto* second edition, one which has been road-tested and honed with crowdsourced feedback before it has even been published. Lucky you!

Seriously though, this book is dedicated to all those authors who shared their data with me, their tips and tricks, as well as their frustrations. You made this book. Perhaps not in a copyright-muddying, royalty-triggering sense—my lawyer suggests noting—but in all the other ways I can't be sued for when I sell ten million copies.

Finally, my thanks go to Ivča for not throwing me out the window.

Made in the USA
San Bernardino, CA
24 March 2019